THE
BIBLICAL CALENDAR
THEN AND NOW

Will the REAL Calendar Please Stand UP?

Comparing and Contrasting
Holy Scripture to the Dead Sea Scrolls

BILL AND KAREN BISHOP

WingSpan Press

Published in the United States and the United Kingdom
by WingSpan Press, Livermore, CA

The WingSpan name, logo and colophon are the trademarks of WingSpan Publishing.

Publisher's Cataloging-in-Publication data

Names: Bishop, Bill, 1955-, author. | Bishop, Karen, 1950-, author.
Title: The Biblical calendar then and now : will the real calendar please stand up? / Bill and Karen Bishop.
Description: "Comparing and Contrasting Holy Scripture to the Dead Sea Scrolls" |
Livermore, CA: Wingspan Press, 2018.
Identifiers: ISBN 978-1-59594-624-9 (pbk.) | 978-1-59594-937-0 (ebook)
Subjects: LCSH Bible--Criticism, interpretation, etc. | Time in the Bible. | Time--Biblical teaching. | Church year--History. | Church calendar. | BISAC RELIGION / Biblical Studies / General | RELIGION / Biblical Commentary / General | RELIGION / Biblical Criticism & Interpretation / General
Classification: LCC BS680.T54 .B57 2018 | DDC 263--dc23

Second edition 2019

Printed in the United States of America

www.wingspanpress.com

Library of Congress Control Number: 2018945326

1 2 3 4 5 6 7 8 9 10

ACKNOWLEDGMENTS

This journey has been arduous, and support has been marginal at best. That is often the case when something new emerges, and it is seen as a threat to the established norm. However, there has been considerable support from some who have followed this research, and not only seen the validity of it, but have realized the significant impact to come as its understanding unfolds. These few folks have been a bulwark to us during this process, and we are deeply indebted to their backing, their input, and their encouragement. Most of all, we are grateful to our Heavenly Father, who has faithfully upheld us through the moments of turmoil, and has showed us the way to pull all of this together. All glory goes to none other than Him!

CONTEXTUAL NOTES

Be a Berean:

We regard Scripture as God's Word of Truth; and we go to great lengths to be sure that our writings are aligned to His word. However, we are not infallible. Please check our book against the Scriptures to be sure we do not conflict in any way – even as those of Berea did in the days of Paul, per Acts 17:10-11. If a Biblical discrepancy comes to light, please advise us of your thoughts for our evaluation. You will find contact information in the Epilogue. Your comments are welcome.

Biblical Version and Manner of Quotations:

All Biblical verses are quoted from the authorized King James Version (KJV). Any bolding or underlining within these verses is our own added emphasis. Scriptural quotations will not contain either italicized or red lettering notations (as might be found in some Bibles). All quotations from non-Biblical sources are individually credited and italicized for easy identification.

Names for the Father and the Son:

It is important to realize that the Bible is not an American document and was not written by English-speaking people. The Almighty inspired men from other ages to record its wealth of information. It is a Middle Eastern document written by Middle Eastern men who are primarily of Hebraic origin with a Hebraic perspective. Accordingly, when referring to the Father and the Son by their proper names, we (to the best of our ability to determine them) use the names from the original Hebrew language.

Our English Bibles typically substitute "the LORD" (using all upper case) for the proper name of the Father, and the Son is referenced as Jesus. In reality, even the Greek name for Jesus relates back to its Hebrew origin. So - while we will leave verse quotations unchanged in that respect, we will otherwise use what we see as the proper Hebrew names for the Father and the Son in our writing. We will refer to **Yahweh** (instead of "the LORD") and **Y'shua** (instead of Jesus) when we address the Father and the Son respectively by their proper names. We hope this will not offend the reader.

DISCLAIMER

It is needful for us to state that this book is not meant to be a complete theological dissertation regarding the Biblical calendar. Although we believe we have presented a reasonable amount of research and study, we also realize the need for more authoritative and exhaustive academic work. Our intention is to provide a practicable body of evidence that will spur further revelation through constructive dialogue, study and debate on this topic among sincere believers of the Torah.

It is our ardent desire to seek the Truth of our Heavenly Father. Likewise, we pray for His wisdom to guide each of us, the layman and the scholar alike. As we have endeavored to allow Him to show us the way of understanding, we ask that you, the reader, will attempt to honestly and scrupulously consider our presentation in this book. We urge you to carefully and prayerfully evaluate the Scriptural and historical evidence with us, and be prepared to "unearth" notions that appear truthful, yet are, perhaps, nothing more than erroneous traditions of men.

We pray with a great deal of hope that this book can be a balm of Gilead (perpetual fountain, testimony, witness) of sorts.

Jeremiah 8:22
(22) Is there no balm in Gilead; is there no physician there? why then is not the health of the daughter of my people recovered?

Please know that we do not see this as being yet another controversial calendar to further divide the brethren. It is meant to provide a sound foundation of substance in lieu of assumptions and strongly held traditions as our basis for understanding. It is our ultimate goal to bring unity and healing to the arbitrary divisions that afflict Torah-loving brethren - to unravel the conflicting opinions regarding the Biblical calendar, and to bring consolidation under Father's enduring Truth.

Proverbs 24:13-14
(13) My son, eat thou honey, because it is good; and the honeycomb, which is sweet to thy taste:
(14) So shall the knowledge of wisdom be unto thy soul: when thou hast found it, then there shall be a reward, and thy expectation shall not be cut off.

TABLE OF CONTENTS

CHAPTER 1

CALENDAR KEEPING METHODOLOGY

Because there was considerable confusion regarding Yahweh's feast dates in 2016, we embarked on some research to determine the truth of the matter. The path would get more complex by the day, but the breadcrumbs would lead to some results that were extremely enlightening, and this book was born.

The Luni-Solar System

Generally speaking, the Jewish people, as well as those of the Hebrew Roots and Messianic persuasion, use a calendar that is primarily lunar in nature. It is actually considered to be soli-lunar. The "soli" aspect of this calendar means that the sun is also considered when the lunar calendar moves from one year to another. Since the lunar year is shorter than the solar year, the lunar year is brought back into alignment with the solar year by adding a month to the calendar every few years. Accordingly, the standard year has 12 months, but some years have 13 months.

However, this lunar calendar formation is far from being cut and dried today. Lunar months are those in which the start of each new month is determined by the cycle of the moon. Lunar-based calendars are built around these lunar months, but there is disagreement regarding what part of the lunar cycle to use to begin these months. Likewise, the means used to determine the timing for the transition into a new year for this type of calendar is highly disputed.

The lunar methodologies vary widely, ranging from using the full moon as the "new moon" to start the month, to a system that actually starts both a new month and a new week at the "new moon". This latter method is usually referred to as the "lunar Sabbath" system. We will discuss it more later, but for now we will simply mention that it often leaves a partial week that is never completed at the end of the month. Then an entirely new week is started when the new month begins at the "new moon". It, therefore, fails to account for an exact seven-day span between the weekly Sabbaths, and it actually causes the weekly Sabbath to be on various days of the week from one month to the next.

We have worked to compare and contrast all of the known means for soli-lunar calendar determination, and we will now share with you in more detail our findings for the three most common methods.

The Astronomical Conjunction Method

Many conclude that the specific timing of the birth of the new moon cycle should be the actual timing for the birth of the new month. They see the moon as being "born" at the precise timing of the alignment of the moon, the sun, and the Earth. Therefore, it is "new" at that moment in time. Though the moon is not yet visible from Earth's perspective, they believe the moon and the sun provide the two witnesses to Father from His perspective during this alignment process. Accordingly, they see this alignment as the decree from Father that the "new moon" has occurred and the new month is to begin. So – this alignment is the demarcation that ends each old month and begins the new according to this system.

The conjunction method is determined today by astronomical data. We have easy access today to the astronomical data that gives us the explicit timing for this alignment. Since there is regularity in the movement of the moon, this data is compiled for the future, as well as for the past and the present. It is actually available years in advance of the actual event.

Those who use this method usually also use astronomical data relative to the spring equinox to determine when to start of the new calendar and when to add the extra month to the year.

Even within this general method, there are different approaches as to how to apply this data, particularly as it relates to the start of the new year. This means that there may be variance between one calendar and another, even using the conjunction method. Once a method is determined for any individual or group though, this type of calendar offers the distinct advantage of having access to the data needed to determine and/or print calendars in advance. People can then know in advance when to observe all of Yahweh's holy feast days.

The Sighting Method

We recall that the conjunction occurs at the exact timing of the alignment of the moon with the Earth and the sun. This alignment puts the Earth between the moon and the sun. Since the moon reflects the light of the sun, the Earth blocks the light source to the moon. As a result, the moon has nothing to reflect for a brief span of time, and it appears dark to us here on Earth. Those who adhere to the sighting method of the "new moon" to start their months, believe that the moon is not to be considered "new" until it has emerged from its dark state of the alignment and its reflection of the sun's rays can once again be seen by us here on Earth. Using this method, the visible sighting of the first sliver of the moon's light after its dark stage (called the waxing crescent) determines the timing for the new month.

Due to the movement of the moon around the Earth and the Earth around the sun, the amount of time it appears dark from our perspective can vary from month to month. It can be anywhere from 1-1/2 to 3-1/2 days. Roughly half of that would be the time from the astronomical conjunction until the first light of the new moon can be seen from earth. Therefore, it may be 1 or 2 days after the conjunction before the first light of the emerging moon can be seen. This makes this type of calendar about one to two days behind the conjunction calendar on a fairly regular basis. The first visible light of the new moon will be a mere sliver of light, which is not always easy to spot. Typically, the new month is not officially begun until two authorized people sight it and make a formal declaration that the new month has begun. What constitutes "authorized" is disputable in this method, and even the need for the second witness comes into question by some.

The Karaite Jews are famous for their lunar observations from Israel. They are often considered to be the authority for determining when to begin the new months. Many rely entirely upon their judgment, and they await notification from the Karaites to begin the new month. Others make their own observations. As a result, the timing for the new month can vary from one locale to another, particularly when people using this method are on opposite sides of the globe. The sighting method is so subjective that even next-door neighbors can start their months on different days if they rely on their own personal observations. As long as communication is open and freely accessible, many will probably continue to use Karaite criteria. However, if that changes, there may be no way to be informed of their determinations. The fact that many different individual sighting methods and locations are used means there is little unity for adherents of this method. No matter whether the Karaite authority is honored or personal observation is used, the need for visual observation makes it virtually impossible to plan festival celebrations in advance.

A further complication with this method is atmospheric conditions. There are times when the new sliver would be visible, but there is too much cloud cover to spot it. Those who use this method bow to the factor of time in such cases, and if sighting is still not possible when it is necessary to advance the calendar, a new month is declared without the sighting. Once the starting date for a new month is determined, then the timing for any of Yahweh's holy feast days that occur within that month can be affixed to the calendar.

A distinct down-side to this method is the inability to determine Yahweh's holy feast days in advance. For instance, the Feast of Trumpets is to be a day of rest and one is not to labor at his routine job. This day always falls on the 1st day of the 7th month. If the moon must be sighted to determine which day starts the 7th month, then it is impossible to plan ahead which day one will need to take off from his job to honor this holy day properly. Likewise, it is impossible to schedule vacation time for the week of the Feast of Tabernacles with enough advanced notice to suit most employers. Though the date for any new month can be forecast to be a specific day, it can never be determined for sure in advance, as the ability to sight the first sliver of the moon will remain uncertain.

For those who employ this visual method for determining the new month, the timing for beginning the new year is usually determined in a visual manner as well. If barley is found to be "abib" at the end of the twelfth month, the new year begins. If it is not, an extra month is added. The "abib" stage of barley is when the barley is no longer dark and has begun to stiffen and develop golden streaks. When they find barley that fits this criteria at the end of the twelfth month, they realize that it should be ready at the right time to be waved at the first fruits harvest, so they determine that the new year will begin. If the barley is not found to be "abib" at the end of the twelfth month, they see the need for extra ripening time, and a 13th month is added before starting the new year.

The Karaite Jews are also famous for doing "abib" barley searches in Israel. The judgment relative to the sighting of the barley can be a tricky matter. Someone with the knowledge to determine the onset of "abib" by visual means must be dispatched for the search. The determination as to how much (if any) of the barley actually fits the "abib" category has to be made. Barley matures faster in some regions than others, even within the same country. Its maturity can even depend on altitude, creating deviation within the same field. As a result, many folks who believe in this method look entirely to the judgment of the Karaite Jews relative to the start of the new calendar year. Again though, if communication becomes problematic, how are people supposed to know what has been determined? As in the sighting of the new moon, others also make their own observations, whether in Israel or abroad. However, some regions do not even grow barley, so there is nothing to refer to for local (much less individual) observation. As a result, the timing for the new year can also vary from one locale to another, or it would be delayed until information is received.

Some years (such as we experienced in 2016), there is considerable disagreement among various groups and individuals regarding whether or not the barley is "abib". Indeed, in 2016 the result did vary from one location to another, and the calendar for some who used this method was not just off by a day here and there, but by an entire month. Unfortunately, the very nature of determining the new month and the new year with the necessity of visual observation is laden with a tremendous amount of subjectivity. As a result, the inconsistencies associated with it have wrought a great deal of confusion in the timing for observation of Yahweh's holy feast days. Because such vast diversity exists within this method, there is little uniformity of feast dates, and it is often difficult for bodies of Believers to discern when to meet together to honor them.

The Hillel Method

Another version of soli-lunar calendar keeping is called Hillel. Information about the Hillel name is sketchy to say the least. Piecing together various references from several encyclopedic sources, it looks as though the first publicized figure named Hillel was actually Babylonian by birth and received his initial education there. Also known as Hillel Hazaken, or Hillel the Elder, this man was later able (at the time of King Herod) to spend the prime of his life studying in Jerusalem. He was then privileged to head the Sanhedrin of his day. The Sanhedrin was the Rabbinical body that had always been accepted as decision makers relative to calendar matters.

With Hillel the Elder, the Hillel Dynasty came into being. This dynasty would form much of the spirit and quality of the Judaism we know today. There were some intervening generations between Hillel the Elder and Hillel II, but throughout the years, the dynasty continued to prosper. Hillel the II (also known as Hillel the Nasi or simply as Hillel) also presided over the Jewish Sanhedrin. It was at his death in 365 A.D. that the prestigious Hillel dynasty finally ended. The crowning achievement of Hillel II was the formation of his Hillel calendar. He had become increasingly aware that the Sanhedrin was about to be dissolved, and he realized the need to develop a calendar that would require little intervention to determine times. Along with some others in Rabbinical capacity, he pulled together what is known and used today as the Hillel calendar.

While this calendar considers the calculated arrival of the first crescent phase of the moon, it does not require the sighting of it. The crescent moon aspect is blended with some rather complex structuring of other Rabbinical criteria. While most of the months of the Hillel calendar have pre-determined lengths, two of them do not. The months which do not, allow the Sanhedrin the flexibility they need to make adjustments (sometimes called postponements) in order to prevent the 1st day of the fall feasts from falling on certain days of the week.

This calendar originated with Hillel, hence its name. The Hillel calendar is now published and made available to the public as a source of authority to determine the start of months and years, as well as the timing of Yahweh's feast days. It is laid out for years into the future, so one can browse online to find the data far in advance of any future dates. At least those who use this method can plan for the observance of the feast days in time to make all necessary arrangements.

CHAPTER 2

PROBLEMS COMING INTO VIEW

We were getting a pretty good grip on the different methodologies in use today, but it seemed that the Father's Holy Days for the year 2016 would come either too early if the extra month was not added, or too late if it was. The proper timing of the harvests could be problematic in either case. Was that REALLY Father's intent?

Too Long, Too Short

The year 2016 was a very strange year, and a prime example of the difficulties that arise from having an entire month variance from one year to the next. It seemed that if people added the month to their year that their barley would be ripe too early for the wave offering of first fruits. If they did not add the extra month, the timing for the wave offering would arrive before the harvest was ready. Variance of a full 1-month span of time seemed to be too extreme, whichever way it went. The ideal timing based on barley maturity would have been to start the new year between the two options. The calendar does NOT determine the timing for the barley harvest. The sun is responsible for that. The calendar is to be adjusted to the actual timing of the sun so the harvest will occur at the proper time of the calendar year. The timing for the barley harvest and the week of Unleavened Bread which is associated with it must be closely knit to the proper amount of heat and light from the sun. Unleavened Bread is fixed to a specific time in the 1st month of the calendar year, so the timing for the beginning of that month on the calendar is critical. The month Yahweh calls "Abib" in Exodus 12:2 is the month when the barley is to ripen to its "abib" stage. For this to happen the amount of heat and light from the sun must be just right to produce this stage of maturity. The sun's heat and light are inadequate for proper barley maturity if the 1st month of the year begins too early. Conversely, the sun's heat and light are more intense when the beginning of the year is too late, and the barley harvest is ready too early for the wave sheaf offering. The choice of whether or not to extend the exiting year by one month before beginning the new year is a very important one.

It is critical to remember that man's calendars do not dictate the heat and light of the sun. Accordingly, neither do man's calendars dictate the readiness of the crops. The crops are governed only by Yahweh's actual seasons. The adjustments of man's calendars must conform to those conditions. If man's calendars are adjusted improperly, the dating on them will NOT match the reality of Father's seasons, and the crops will be ready at the improper times for His agricultural based festivals.

In making these adjustments, it is typically thought that there is only one concern - the maturity of the barley. However, we find that there are other concerns. If the extra month is applied incorrectly or not applied when it should have been, the fall festivals are also affected. The fall harvest which is linked to Feast of Tabernacles is fixed to a specific time in the 7th month of the calendar year. Because the months continue in straight-forward fashion, the improper maturity stage of the barley may be only the beginning of the problem. The issue can become even worse when the fall festivals arrive.

If the month is not added, the calendar may place the spring feasts too early, and the fall feasts will come too early as well. The fall crops may be just ready for harvest or in progress of harvest when the ardent Jew will have to abandon the fields for more than a week to go to Jerusalem for Feast of Tabernacles. On the other hand, if the 13th month is added, not only might the calendar bring in the spring feasts too late, but the fall feasts will be too late as well. The ingathering harvest may occur a bit too early for the Feast of Tabernacles festivities. Though it is not stated Biblically, the implication is that the produce should be fresh when it graces the tables of the feast.

In years like 2016, there are typically problems whether or not the extra month is added. If the extra month is not added, it may be possible by some stretch to eke out enough barley to form a sheaf for waving in the spring. However, the timing for Feast of Tabernacles in the fall would likely be problematic. If the extra month is added, the Feast of Tabernacles may be somewhat manageable, yet the barley may no longer be proper for the wave sheaf offering of the spring feasts.

At times like the year of 2016 a whole month (about 1/12 of an entire year) seems to be too lengthy a span of time to use in adjusting the year. If only it had been proper to adjust the calendar year by just a week or two, it would have been fine. That simply is not a viable option though – or is it? To see how there might be another option, we must dissect some of the core beliefs which compose the calendar methods shown above. As we proceed, we may find that there is not only another valid option, but that much needs to be addressed about the current understanding of Yahweh's calendar timing.

CHAPTER 3

RETURNING TO THE SOURCE

In order to get to the source of Father's truth, we felt it necessary to go back to what was originally written – before English translators intervened. We went back to the disposition within the language of the original manuscript. When we explored the etymology of the Hebrew wording, an entirely new world of understanding opened up to us.

Chodesh

The backbone of all three of the methods above is that the new month begins with the "new moon". The wording "new moon" or "new moons" is used 20 times in our KJV Old Testament. The term that is translated as "new moon" is always the same Hebrew word: "chodesh". Likewise, without exception, the plural ("new moons") is always the plural form of "chodesh" ("chodeshim"). (The "im" at the end of the word designates its plural form.) It is Strong's H2320 - *the new moon, month; monthly; the first day of the month; the lunar month*. The term "chodesh" is one of the more fascinating and confusing Hebrew terms in the Bible. Actually, only a few passages in the Old Testament have translated this Hebrew word as "new moon(s)", and in those cases, the English rendering of the Biblical text does make it seem that these "new moons" might be the determining factor for the new months. Before we lock onto that though, a little more research on this term might be helpful.

Notably, Strong's illustrates here that the word "chodesh" does not always include the lunar aspect. It can simply mean month, monthly, or the 1st day of the month. Further research shows us that "chodesh" or a variation of it (such as "chodeshim") is used some 71 times throughout the first 5 books of the Bible, the writings of Moses, or Torah. In this portion of the Word it is always translated as "month(s)" - never being linked to the moon at all. These Biblical records of the teachings of Moses include no instruction whatsoever relative to a lunar-based calendar system, nor do they ever indicate that the calendar he used had anything to do with the moon.

Why do we have the two different translations for "chodesh(im)" - Torah containing only one translation, but a different translation being used occasionally in the other Old Testament books? What might the full Hebraic implications of this word be? Could the Hebrew manuscripts show us something that our English translation does not? Our concordance and lexical aids are steadfast tools in our reference libraries, but do they provide the total extent of the options for any given Hebrew word? Furthermore, from what sources are their definitions derived? Our <u>Strong's Exhaustive Concordance of the Bible</u> is dedicated to Dr. James Strong, who lived from 1822-1894. That was a long while after the first writing of the King James Bible in 1611. Is it possible that the definitions this book presents were at least partially derived from the work of English Biblical translators? Accordingly, what if there is reasonable cause to doubt the manner in which our English text had been translated? Is it possible that the choice for certain words that were used in our English translations of the Bible simply reflect the Jewish practices of that day rather than the application of the ancient Hebrew

Scripture? Could the lunar-based calendar which has been observed in Israel for more than 2,000 years be the persuading factor for using "new moon" as the translation of choice for some of our English Biblical text, and also have led to the choice of that wording among the definitions in our lexicons as well? Could this in turn have created a rift in the true Hebraic intent of certain passages? Let's put on our waders and explore the fluid etymology of this word!

Hebrew letters have meanings. Elemental to the study of etymology is the breaking down of the Hebrew word into its individual letters to see what each of these letters mean. This, in turn, provides insight about the meaning and Yahweh-inspired intention of the word as a whole. A compilation of several sources was used to present the following etymological information about "chodesh":

Its letter structure is chet, dalet, shin.

The letter "chet" means: *the new beginning of transcendent life, chamber, private, separate, outside, divide, half.*

The letter "dalet" means: *the way of the open door, move, hang, enter.*

The letter "shin" means: *divine providence, full cycle, consume, destroy, fire, sharp, press, eat, two.*

Therefore, we see an action represented in this word: progression through a door from the end of a cycle to the beginning of a new cycle. This revolving door will repeat at the conclusion of each cycle to bring renewal.

"Chodesh" stems from the root word Strong's H2318 (chadash) - *to be new, renew, repair; to renew, make anew.* This too shows the process of the cycle, with the renewal of the process on a regular basis. Another related Hebrew word is Strong's H2319 (chadash) - *new, new thing, fresh.* It has the same transliterated spelling as H2318. All three words are tightly related.

It is worthy of note that the Hebrew term "chodesh(im)" is used 276 times in the Bible. Only 20 times is it translated as "new moon(s)", while 254 times it is translated as "month(s)" and once as "monthly". One remaining time it is translated as "another" (Esther 9:19), where it also relates to "month".

Examining the 20 times the Bible translates "chodesh(im)" as "new moon(s)", there really is no instance when the idea of the start of a month or the associated celebration would not be appropriate instead. Note that some might challenge a definition of "month" as it relates to Psalm 81:3 where "chodesh" has been translated as "new moon":

Psalms 81:3
(3) Blow up the trumpet in the new moon, in the time appointed, on our solemn feast day.

However, this verse, as well as other significant points regarding "chodesh" will be covered as we proceed.

Yareach

The Hebrew language has an entirely different word that actually means moon. It is Strong's H3394 (yareach). For this particular word, there is only one meaning listed in Strong's, which is - *moon.* That might be because it is used 26 times in the Biblical text, and it is never translated as anything but "moon". There is no confusion when this word is used. It is always clearly the lunar object in the sky that provides our light at night.

We have found that the term "chodesh" in and of itself simply indicates a transition that concludes a cycle and begins a new one. The question for any particular passage would be what type of cyclical transition is being indicated.

If the Hebrew manuscripts had intended "new moon(s)" to be the understood meaning for the 20 times "chodesh(im)" is translated "new moon(s)", the author of the manuscript could easily have used "yareach" (the word for "moon") in conjunction with "chadash" (a word for "new" as is differentiated above from "chodesh"). This then would specify that the lunar object in the sky was in its "new" phase.

It seems that if this cyclical change was in reference to something as tangible and simplistic as the moon, the word for moon ("yareach") would almost assuredly be used somewhere in the nearby context of the Hebrew manuscript itself. That would allow for the passage to be cut and dried. The fact that the manuscript does not contain the word "yearach" in these passages, actually carries the heavy implication that these designated "chodesh" transitions are NOT relative to the moon at all.

There is one verse in which "yareach" is used that was a bit problematic when we initially confronted it. It seemed to show that the actual moon does indeed have a special role in determining times. The verse is found in Psalms:

Psalms 104:19
(19) He appointed the moon for seasons: the sun knoweth his going down.

The word "seasons" in this verse is Strong's H4150 (mow`ed) - *appointed place, appointed time, meeting; appointed time (general), sacred season, set feast, appointed season; appointed place, appointed sign or signal, tent of meeting*. Obviously, not all of these are meant at any one time. Some use this verse to show that the "moon" is appointed to determine the festivals (appointed sacred seasons). If this is so, the reasoning evolves that it must be the moon that determines the start of the months, which in turn dictates the timing for these festivals. There is a bit of a flaw in this thought process though. In order for this interpretation to be valid, it must be removed from its context. Let's look at the context of this verse:

Psalms 104:19-22
(19) He appointed the moon for seasons: the sun knoweth his going down.
(20) Thou makest darkness, and it is night: wherein all the beasts of the forest do creep forth.
(21) The young lions roar after their prey, and seek their meat from God.
(22) The sun ariseth, they gather themselves together, and lay them down in their dens.

This clearly indicates that the moon is appointed to be the "mow`ed" (sign or signal) for the onset of the night portion of the 24-hour days. It is merely the "sign or signal" aspect of the definition for "mow`ed" that applies here. The context of this passage in no way links this use of "mow`ed" to the festivals or holy day seasons, or to the extended aspect of determining the onset of the months in which those festivals are to occur. In fact, a further study of "yareach" showed us that the moon is primarily appointed as a sign or faithful witness to the sun. It is almost always used in a context involving the sun, and a passage from Psalm 89 shows it is a powerful witness:

Psalms 89:36 & 37
(36) His seed shall endure for ever, and his throne as the sun before me.
(37) It shall be established for ever as the moon, and as a faithful witness in heaven. Selah.

When the moon ("yareach") is referenced Biblically, it is as a light with the dedicated role of dividing day from night, and that is its only timing function. Even its mention as a faithful "`ed" (witness) in Psalms 89:37 is in association with the sun to fulfill this same role. There is no doubt that it could be designated as a "sign" ("mow`ed" or "`owth") in conjunction with "chodesh", but that simply never happens. The moon might be loosely characterized as a sign of sorts in Joel, Acts, and Revelation when it is prophesied to become "as blood". However, there is simply no such "sign" related to the routine lunar changes of phases, and such lunar phase variation is certainly never mentioned in association with "chadosh" in any reference of the Hebrew Biblical manuscript.

There is actually **only one** Biblical reference that even vaguely implies observance of the changes in the phases of the moon ("yareach"). It is found in Job 31:26-28:

Job 31:26-28
(26) If I beheld the sun when it shined, or the moon walking in brightness;
(27) And my heart hath been secretly enticed, or my mouth hath kissed my hand:
(28) This also were an iniquity to be punished by the judge: for I should have denied the God that is above.

Job indicates that beholding the moon "walking in brightness" is a highly questionable practice! In his wisdom, he implies here that following the lunar changes could actually lead him into a punishable offense. His reference to denial of God in verse 28 may actually imply association of this type of lunar observation to pagan practice.

The references in Torah (and the Old Testament at large) to "chodesh(im)" as "month(s)" may not always be a choice translation either though, as the etymology of "chodesh(im)" indicates that it could actually relate to virtually any cycle and/or transition in time, including seasons or years - depending on the surrounding context. This could vary from one location in the Word to another, or even imply multiple cyclical and/or transitional events in a single passage, to be determined by the context where "chodesh(im)" is found.
Particularly relative to the 20 usages of "chodesh(im)" translated as "new moon(s)" though, we now suspect that the translators of our English text were merely heeding the influence associated with rabbinic tradition of that day, rather than adhering to the more precise translation that the manuscripts may have warranted. This will become clearer as we proceed.

CHAPTER 4

THE LUNAR AND SOLAR DISCREPANCY

Next, we had to confront the ever-perplexing issue of the imbalance of the duration of solar year to that of the lunar year. No matter how much we want them to correlate perfectly, the fact is that they simply do not. How are we to compensate for this difference when trying to formulate God's Biblical calendar?

In Sync or Out of Sync?

Some researchers have come to the conclusion that the sun, the moon, and the month were originally in sync with one another at the time of their creation. Actually, it is thought that our English word "month" might have originally been derived from the word "moon" - something like "moonth". It is believed that there were 360 days in a year, 12 months of exactly 30 days each. The moon was thought to take precisely 30 days to rotate around the earth, and the earth was to take precisely 360 days to rotate around the sun. This would explain much about the association between new moons and months. In his book, Worlds in Collision, Immanuel Velikovsky wrote of numerous ancient cultures that recorded 30-day months. Whether 30 days was the average duration of the typical month or a precise measure of time is not clear. What does seem to be clear is the strong association between the number 30 and the month.

In like manner, piecing together a couple of timing passages in Genesis should make us stop and take note. Noah was afloat in the ark for 5 months. The wording in Genesis is actually very specific:

Genesis 7:11, 8:3-4
(11) In the six hundredth year of Noah's life, in the **second month, the seventeenth day** of the month, the same day were all the fountains of the great deep broken up, and the windows of heaven were opened.
(3) And the waters returned from off the earth continually: and **<u>after</u> the end of the hundred and fifty days** the waters were abated.
(4) And the ark rested in the **seventh month, on the seventeenth day** of the month, upon the mountains of Ararat.

Note that the span of time was from the 17th day of the 2nd month to the 17th day of the 7th month. It was the same day of the month, 5 months later when the ark came to rest. If these months were 30 days each, the 17th day of the 7th month would actually be the 151st day from the 17th day of the 2nd month. Some indicate though that the word "after" in this passage leaves room for the speculation that there might even have been slightly more than 150 days in this 5-month period, that there is the potential for extra days to be a part of the equation, allowing for some months to be more than 30 days. We will see later how that could be of importance. The important thing to consider now though, is that there were <u>at least</u> 150 days in this span of time.

An interesting consideration is the manner in which any lunar-based calendar system is orchestrated today. There is only a mixture of 29 and 30-day months throughout the year. There are sometimes two 30-day months in a row. There are rarely three, almost never four, and no evidence whatsoever for five 30-day con-secutive months on any current version of the Jewish lunar calendar system. If the sun and moon actually WERE totally in sync at that time, it could have been 30-day months, based on both the lunar and the solar timing. However, if the differential between the solar and the lunar cycles was much as it is today, then it seems that the number of days in a month must have been attributed to some type of solar-based calendar system which would have months that were at least 30-days each. It does not appear to be at all possible for the 5-month period that spanned at least (and possibly slightly more than) 150 days to have been relative to our current version of the lunar calendar system.

It is not our purpose to concretely determine whether or not the lunar and solar years were once in sync. However, we do wish to establish that even if they once were, it is apparent that they no longer are. Presently, in 2017, a trip of the Earth around the sun takes 365 days, 5 hours, 55 minutes, and 12 seconds, or 365.24667 days. The lunar cycle averages 29.530587981 days. A 12-lunar cycle year would then be about 354.367055772 days. This is 10.879614228 days before the solar cycle concludes. This means that the lunar year is some 10 days shorter than the solar year.

The Bible repeatedly infers that the month is to be viewed as 30-day intervals. The end of a lunar cycle occurs .469412019 days before a complete 30-day Biblical month would conclude. That is about half a day variance, which is the reason roughly half of the Jewish lunar months are only 29 days long, while the other half have a 30-day duration. The moon cycle is now emphatically out of sync with the Biblical month. If indeed the lunar and solar years ever were identical and interchangeable, they are no longer so.

Relativity of Monthly Timing to Chodesh

Returning to the Hebrew word "chodesh" we see that it lends to both the concept of moon and month, as both are progressive from the new or renewed state to the conclusion of a cycle and the start of another. Accordingly, it is often presumed today that the moon cycle and the monthly cycle are somewhat inter-changeable. Yet, it should be coming apparent that this is not possible, as the lunar cycle and the 30-day Scriptural month no longer align with each other. As we have just illustrated, there is roughly a half day dif-ferential between the average lunar month and the Biblical month, and yet a further differential of some 10 days between the solar and lunar year.

The Need for Intercalation

"Intercalation" is the term used when the length of a calendar year is adjusted by adding extra days (or on the lunar calendar, an extra month) in order to realign with the actual solar year. All calendars must be adjusted periodically to synchronize again with the precise solar aspect of the sky overhead. It seems ob-vious then that one of two things will need to happen between now and the fulfillment of some prophetic passages in Revelation. In order for 1260 days, 3-1/2 years, and 42 months to represent the same period of time, either Yahweh must readjust the timing of the cycle for the solar year to 360, (and possibly the lunar year as well), OR the days that are added for intercalation (adjustment) will simply not be reckoned in these calculations. The intercalary days will just be disregarded, taking into account only the days of the basic calendar structure.

Some cultures have rendered the term "out of time" for such intercalary days. The Mayans have a complex calendar system which considers numerous counts of varying lengths. By combining their multiple versions of calendars, their ability to track time has been accounted as one of the most precise and accurate method of keeping time throughout history. Two of these calendars (the 13 Moon and the Haab) both incorporate these days "out of time" very effectively around their precise calendar frameworks. Such days are merely inserted as an intercalary measure to adjust the standard calendar framework to the solar year. "Out of time" simply means that the placement of these intercalary days is designed to fulfill time constraints while enhancing the continuity for the framework of time that forms that calendar.

Even our own calendar is adjusted in this manner almost every 4th year by adding an intercalary day "out of time" or "leap" day. Generally speaking, these days are treated as though they do not really exist. February is still normally considered to be a 28-day month. Our Gregorian year is thought to be 365 days, even though it is 366 days about 25% of the time.

Intercalation and Agriculture

The barley ripens in accordance with the sun, so if the lunar calendar is used to provide the dating for the Feast of Unleavened Bread and the associated waving of the first fruits barley sheaf, periodic intercalation adjustments must be made to the calendar. If no periodic adjustments were made to the moon-based calendar to bring it into harmony with the sun-based calendar, calendar dates would regress. Observation of the Feast of Unleavened Bread would eventually come during the frigid cold of winter, back through the fall, then into the blazing heat of summer, before coming full cycle back to the spring. How would one wave the barley in the off seasons when no barley is available? Yahweh's calendar is agriculturally based:

Genesis 8:22
(22) While the earth remaineth, seedtime and harvest, and cold and heat, and summer and winter, and day and night shall not cease.

If the lunar calendar is used, intercalation MUST be made to keep the calendar in the proper time-frame with the harvests. This is not only vital to all lunar calendars, but even solar calendars like our Gregorian must make slight adjustments to accommodate the odd timing of the precise solar year.

Agriculture and Reality

We have referenced the agricultural nature of Yahweh's calendar. Whereas the moon has little to do with the growing seasons, the sun is an indisputable factor in the agricultural framework. The seasons are reckoned by the action of the sun. The growth of plant life is incrementally linked to the duration of sunlight and heat of the sun. The heavens display and record the movement of the sun from our perspective on Earth. They provide a marker for our transition from winter into spring and then again from summer into fall. This marker is the equinox. According to the Encyclopedia Britannica, the definition of an equinox is:

Encyclopedia Britannica - Equinox - Astronomy - http://www.britannica.com/topic/equinox-astronomy - *Equinox, either of the two moments in the year when the sun is exactly above the equator and day and night are of equal length; also, either of the two points in the sky **where the ecliptic** (the Sun's annual pathway) **and the celestial equator** intersect.*

The International Encyclopedia of Astronomy defines the celestial equator as:

The International Encyclopedia of Astronomy - edited by Patrick Moore – p. 93 –
... an equatorial circle that is equidistant from the poles and touches the horizon due east and due west. ...

a projection of the Earth's equator onto the celestial sphere and is our view of the plane passing through the centre of the Earth and dividing the sky into two hemispheres.

Psalms somewhat cryptically records this process:

Psalms 19:4-6
(4) **Their line is gone out through all the earth**, and their words to the end of the world. In them hath he set a <u>tabernacle for the sun,</u>
(5) Which is as <u>a bridegroom coming out of his chamber,</u> and rejoiceth as a <u>strong man to run a race.</u>
(6) His going forth is <u>from the end of the heaven,</u> and **his circuit unto the ends of it**: and there is <u>nothing hid from the heat thereof.</u>

The Hebrew word for "line" in verse 4 is Strong's H6957 (qav) - *a cord for measuring; measuring line; a rule.* Regarding this "line", Warren Baker and Eugene Carpenter say:

<u>The Complete Word Study Dictionary Old Testament</u> – by Warren Baker, D.R.E. and Eugene Carpenter, Ph.D. - p. 985 -
It refers to <u>the architectural plan, line, of the heavens that reflects God's work.</u>

Assessing these words, we find that indeed the "line" that goes out through all the earth is recorded as an architectural plan or blueprint in God's heavens. It is further linked to the word "circuit" in verse 6. This word is Strong's H8622 (těquwphah) - *coming round, circuit of time or space; a turning around.* Baker and Carpenter comment on " těquwphah" by saying:

<u>The Complete Word Study Dictionary Old Testament</u> - by Warren Baker, D.R.E. and Eugene Carpenter, Ph.D. - p. 1244 -
It indicates the completion of a yearly cycle. It is used to describe the circuit or passage of the sun across the sky.

The cycle of the movement of the sun across the sky from our perspective is then designated by a line or marker which specifies the start and conclusion of this "circuit". Exodus also clearly relates this same Hebrew word with this yearly circuit, showing the conclusion of the cycle.

Exodus 34:22
(22) And thou shalt observe the feast of weeks, of the firstfruits of wheat harvest, and the feast of ingathering at the **year's end**.

The word for "end" in this verse is also "těquwphah". Psalm 19 indicates that a type of line of demarcation (the celestial equator) extends through all of the earth. Its markers for our seasonal change can be witnessed 2 times of the year (a double witness of sorts) when the ecliptic intersects with it. These 2 times of year are the vernal (spring) equinox and the autumnal (fall) equinox. Devices that measure the shadows of the sun and length of daylight are called sundials. The equinoxes are easily identified using these ancient devices.

Yahweh established in Exodus that His year was to be reckoned by the spring equinox. The month that begins His year is the 1st month after this equinox, and this month is Biblically referenced as Abib (or in some versions Aviv). It is the month when the barley will become Abib (a stage of ripeness), and it will be matured in time for the waving of the sheaf offering. It is the month the people came out of Egypt, the month when the

Passover lambs are to be slain, the month when the week of the Feast of Unleavened Bread is to be honored, and the month when the sheaf of barley is to be waved:

Exodus 12:2.
(2) This month shall be unto you the beginning of months: it shall be the first month of the year to you.

Exodus 12:11
(11) ...it is the LORD's passover.

Exodus 13:4
(4) This day came ye out in the month Abib.

Exodus 34:18
(18) The feast of unleavened bread shalt thou keep. Seven days thou shalt eat unleavened bread, as I commanded thee, in the time of the month Abib: for in the month Abib thou camest out from Egypt.

Leviticus 23:10-11
(10) Speak unto the children of Israel, and say unto them, When ye be come into the land which I give unto you, and shall reap the harvest thereof, then ye shall bring a sheaf of the firstfruits of your harvest unto the priest:
(11) And he shall wave the sheaf before the LORD, to be accepted for you: on the morrow after the sabbath the priest shall wave it.

The Feast of Unleavened Bread is the feast associated with the waving of the first fruits barley sheaf. Thus, the 1st month of Yahweh's year would now be the month when the barley fully ripens (the first crop of the new year) and a first fruits wave offering of this first harvest is commanded. The ripening of barley is predominantly due to the heat and amount of light from the sun being adequate to mature the grain. The line in the sky which correctly indicates the arrival of this season of proper heat and lighting is the vernal (spring) equinox. It marks the end of the previous year's cycle, and the start of the new one.

Referring back again to the Psalms passage above, we would note the "tabernacle set for the sun". We will bring it back for quick reference:

Psalms 19:4-6
(4) Their <u>line</u> is gone out through all the earth, and their words to the end of the world. In them hath he set a <u>tabernacle for the sun</u>,
(5) Which is as a bridegroom coming out of his chamber, and rejoiceth as a strong man to <u>run a race</u>.
(6) His going forth is from the end of the heaven, and his circuit unto the ends of it: and there is nothing hid from the <u>heat thereof</u>.

There are possibly multiple meanings for this rather mysterious passage. However, there are several trigger words within it that point to a potential pattern in Father's Heavens to dictate His calendar. The "line" is the vernal (spring) equinox, the sign that the "sun" (which dictates the proper "heat" for ripening) is here. The "race" is the yearly "circuit" from one vernal equinox to the next. In this same passage, we see that the "line" in verse 4 and the circuit in verse 6 are connected in verse 5 with the "bridegroom coming out of his chamber". What might this tabernacle for the sun be?

CHAPTER 5

STARS ENTER THE PICTURE

We had been working primarily with Father's sun and moon to this point. However, His stars are also a significant part of His celestial handiwork, and we were about to see how they were a part in our emerging picture as well.

Father's Mazzaroth

This may be where the stars come into play. The term "mazzaroth" is a Biblical term used in the book of Job. It relates to the starry host, but more specifically, to the houses and constellations of it. The movement of the "mazzaroth" is associated in Job with the seasons, and it is substantiated as being a part of the "ordinances of heaven":

Job 38:31-33
(31) Canst thou bind the sweet influences of <u>Pleiades</u>, or loose the bands of <u>Orion</u>?
(32) Canst thou bring forth **Mazzaroth** in his **season**? or canst thou guide <u>Arcturus</u> with his sons?
(33) Knowest thou the **ordinances of heaven**? canst thou set the dominion thereof in the earth?

Jeremiah speaks of Yahweh's appointment of these <u>heavenly ordinances</u>, stating that they were put in place <u>by His discretion</u>:

Jeremiah 33:25
(25) Thus saith the LORD; If my covenant be not with day and night, and if I have not <u>appointed the **ordinances of heaven**</u> and earth;

Jeremiah 10:12
(12) He hath made the earth by his power, he hath established the world by his wisdom, and hath <u>stretched out the heavens **by his discretion**</u>.

Astrology is man's philosophy regarding the influence of the stars on man. Astronomy, on the other hand, is Yahweh's revelation to man of His majesty in the heavens and how He provides His timing for His creation below. While astrology is Biblically denigrated because it involves worshiping heavenly bodies, astronomy is actually encouraged in the study of Yahweh's ongoing revelation of Himself to us. While Yahweh calls His heavenly display the "mazzaroth" in Job, astrology uses the term "zodiac". Both relate to the stars in their courses. There are 88 known constellations in Yahweh's mazzaroth. The most prominent groupings of these constellations are known as "houses". Over the procession of time, there has been a slight migration of these constellations in the sky from our earthly perspective (known as the precession of the equinoxes), but astronomically, there is still a link between the mazzaroth and the vernal equinox.

It is still considered to be the time when the sun leaves the house of Pisces and enters the house of Aries. Encyclopedia Britannica actually refers to the vernal equinox as the "first point of Aries":

Encyclopedia Britannica – Aries - https://www.britannica.com/place/Aries -
The first point of Aries, or vernal equinox is an intersection of the celestrial equator with the apparent annual pathway of the Sun ... .

It seems that the houses of the mazzaroth provide an astronomic witness of the vernal equinox as well. The courses of the sun and stars can be quickly and easily researched through accessing an ephemeris (an astronomical table that charts the positions of the sun, the moon, and the planets throughout the year). (An example, and a good resource tool is The Astrolabe World Ephemeris 2001-2050 at Midnight, which provides data regarding the sun, moon, and planets, as well as asteroids.)

Astronomically, these constellations compose 12 "houses" which form the basis of Yahweh's mazzaroth. They are still considered to share the 360-degree circle of our sky with roughly 30-degree segments assigned to each of them.

The number 12 indicates completion with Yahweh. Y'shua had 12 apostles and there were 12 tribes in the lineage of Jacob. Some want to say that Ophiuchus (meaning the serpent) is a 13th house. Each of the 12 astronomical houses cross over the ecliptic. Ophiuchus now partially crosses the ecliptic. For that reason, some reckon it to be a 13th house. However, this actually seems to be irrelevant to the way astronomy classifies the 12 house signs. They divide the ecliptic into equal segments, each one covering 30 degrees of the celestial longitude. This is almost exactly the distance the Sun travels during the month. The sun then enters a new astronomical house roughly every 30 days.

It is interesting that the "serpent" constellation would endeavor to interrupt the continuity Yahweh had designed, suggesting 13 houses rather than His original 12. Just as a side reference, a type of case in point, it seems that the occasional 13th month in the Hebraic calendar which is added to Yahweh's original 12 might well be usurping Yahweh's initial design as well. We'll see more on this later!

Weeks, Months, Seasons, and Years

Putting it all together, these 12 houses and their associated months can be subdivided into 2 groupings of 6, the time between the vernal equinox and the autumnal equinox, then back to the vernal equinox. Between the 2 equinoxes are the 2 solstices. Each of the 4 seasons or 3-month periods is introduced by an equinox or a solstice. These seasonal markers are determined by the sun and the amount of light it provides for our days. The amount of light and darkness during the 24-hour day are virtually equal on equinox days. The day of the winter solstice has the longest period of darkness. Conversely, the day of the summer solstice has the longest period of light. Therefore, the equinoxes mark equal days and nights, and the solstices mark the maximum day and the maximum night.

Each of these quarterly markers signifies the completion of a cycle of time and the beginning of a new one. The Hebrew term "chodesh" is, at the core of its etymology, simply that – the transition into a renewed cycle. We are finding that the four seasonal transitions may actually be the primary focus in reference to "chodeshim", and that the term "seasons" in Genesis 1:14 might actually mean just that – the transitions ("chodeshim") from season to season:

Genesis 1:14

(14) And God said, Let there be lights in the firmament of the heaven to divide the day from the night; and let them be for signs, **and for seasons**, and for days, and years:

The Mazzaroth is indeed a part of Yahweh's lights in His firmament, and the equinox and solstice markers are "signs" that relate to these "seasons". These quarterly markers correspond closely with the start of each literal season, as well as determining the start of the calendar year in the spring. These seasonal markers are not always equidistant from one another, but they are very close to being so, and provide the seasonal transitions. Each equinox and solstice is effectively a line of demarcation which institutes the next season.

CHAPTER 6

THE BROADER SCOPE OF GOD'S HEAVENLY DISPLAY

The scope of Father's heavenly handiwork is amazing; and trying to understand how it was all supposed to fit into the formation of His calendar was challenging to say the least. Yet in spite of the vast nature of His heavenly expanse, the way it all worked together to formulate His timekeeping was becoming more defined as we proceeded. We were getting excited because the depth of meaning in Genesis 1:14 was coming into view!

Cycles and Transition

Considering the value of ALL of Yahweh's patterning, it seems that these seasonal markers are surely and decidedly a part of Yahweh's heavenly array that was established for His timing of the calendar year. They were evidently significant to Noah as well. The Book of Jubilees found in the Dead Sea Scroll fragments documents their significance:

The Book of Jubilees 6:23-28 - The Researchers Library of Ancient Texts Volume 1 - by R.H. Charles, Oxford – p. 288 –
And on the new moon of <u>the first month</u>, and on the new moon of <u>the fourth month</u>, and on the new moon of <u>the seventh month</u>, and on the new moon of <u>the tenth month</u> are the <u>days of remembrance</u>, <u>and the days of the seasons in the four divisions of the year. These are written and ordained as a testimony for ever.</u> And Noah ordained them for himself <u>as feasts</u> for the generations for ever, so that they have become thereby a memorial unto him. And on the new moon of the <u>first month</u> he was bidden to make for himself an ark, and on that (day) the earth became dry and he opened (the ark) and saw the earth. And on the new moon of the <u>fourth month</u> the mouths of the depths of the abyss beneath were closed. And on the new moon of the <u>seventh month</u> all the mouths of the abysses of the earth were opened, and the waters began to descend into them. And on the new moon of the <u>tenth month</u> the tops of the mountains were seen, and Noah was glad. And on this account he ordained them for himself as feasts for a memorial for ever, and thus are they ordained.

We will see later that the translation of "new moon" in this book suffers the same fate as the English versions of the Bible. Since references to "chodesh(im)" were sometimes translated as "new moons" in the Bible, maybe that is why they were likewise translated as "new moons" when the English versions of The Book of Jubilees was drafted. Maybe these references to "new moon(s)" are also simply "days of cyclical transition"; and these cycles could vary from one reference to another - often relating to the cycles of the equinoxes and seasons.

The "chodesh" events of the 1st, 4th, 7th, and 10th months as shown in The Book of Jubilees seem to imply that people are to be gathered together in a memorial celebration of the seasonal transitions they represent. This does not mean that these seasonal transitions carry the same weight as Father's holy days, but it does indicate that they may have a place in His reckoning. There is actually one prominent overlap of Yahweh's holy days and the seasonal "chodesh" days mentioned in The Book of Jubilees. The Biblical Feast of Trumpets is on the 1st day of the 7th month. This is both Father's holy day, and a seasonal marker related to the autumnal equinox. The Biblical reference to The Feast of Trumpets offers the same type of gathering and festival flare that was perhaps enjoyed at these seasonal markers:

Numbers 29:1
(1) And in the seventh month, on the first day of the month, ye shall have an holy convocation; ye shall do no servile work: it is a day of blowing the trumpets unto you.

Though the seasonal transition may not have carried the same significance as the Feast of Trumpets "holy convocation", it would have been a festive gathering of the people in either case. The air would have had a celebratory flare due to the command to abstain from work that day and the blowing of trumpets. This type of overlap seems to indicate that these seasonal transition days also have a somewhat sacred status. Father's orchestration of the significant events in Noah's miraculous journey around these particular times as recorded in The Book of Jubilees further suggests this significance.

On the opposite side of the calendar, Moses was told to erect the Tabernacle at the transition of the year (Exodus 40:2).

Exodus 40:2
(2) On the first day of the first month shalt thou set up the tabernacle of the tent of the congregation.

This occurred at the Spring "chodesh".

In the Days of Moses

There is evidence that the lunar-based calendar as we now know it was not being used in the days of Moses either. He wrote the first five books of our Bible (Torah), and they do not include even the first reference to the "new moon". These books do reference the word "*month*", which is from Strong's H2320 (chodesh), but the idea of moon(s) is not in any way affixed to the word "chodesh(im)" in the five books of Moses. The Bible simply does not directly specify the workings of his calendar, so nothing can be carved in stone about it. Even during the numerous passages relating to the festivals, there is no mention of a "new moon". Since there is no statement regarding a calendar of any sort relative to the days of Moses, we might focus upon what the text does NOT say. There seems to be no lunar aspect whatsoever implied relative to Torah writings. There is never anything mentioned about a crescent-moon sighting, a 29-day month, a short month, or an extra month. This blatant lack of evidence for a lunar-based calendar system may actually add to the implied evidence buried within Scripture of a calendar that is solar-based instead. One thing we can conclude about all of this so far is that the calendar is extremely important to our Heavenly Father, and it also seems quite obscure. He obviously wants us to earnestly and diligently seek His Word, His Way, His Truth, and His Spirit as we come to terms with it. The adversary has put a lot of effort into creating confusion, doubt, and deception surrounding the calendar in order to prevent us from the intimacy of a close relationship with our Abba on His specified feast days. We do not want the enemy to have his way!

Solomon's Equinoctial Temple

What evidence might come to light regarding the use of a solar calendar year in Solomon's day of early Temple times?

Sir Joseph Norman Lockyer was a famous English scientist and astronomer. Numerous writings relative to his work reveal that he studied the orientation of temples and structures to the sun in order to discern equinox and solstice data. Those temples that were oriented to the spring equinox were called "equinoctial". It seems that Solomon's Temple may actually have been equinoctial in its origin. In the virtual library provided by bibliotecapleyades.net, the books by Zechariah Sitchin are made available for research. In his writing, Sitchin referenced the results of Lockyer's work:

When Time Began – The First New Age – Book Five of the Earth Chronicles - by Zechariah Sitchin – courtesy of bibliotecapleyades.net -
http://www.bibliotecapleyades.net/sitchin/sitchinbooks05_02.htm -
As examples of equinoctial temples Lockyer cited the Temple of Zeus at Baalbeck, the Temple of Solomon in Jerusalem, and the great basilica of St. Peter's in the Vatican in Rome - all oriented on a precise east-west axis.

Indeed, Bible History Daily, a Biblical Archaeology Society, has confirmed in their article Searching for the Temple of King Solomon that the east-facing Temple of Solomon in Jerusalem was an equinoctial temple, one that was designed to determine the equinox. The eastern gate was also called the "sun gate". It may have provided not only proper light orientation for the equinoxes, but the solstices as well, so the dating could be easily determined.

Though it is difficult to nail down definitively in Scripture, there is strong implication that the wilderness Tabernacle faced the east also. Those who have studied the wilderness Tabernacle extensively and have even composed detailed diagrams are generally in agreement about the direction it faced. It could be that facing east was part of the "pattern" that Moses was shown in the mount as well.

Once we begin to follow the breadcrumbs, we realize that the lunar calendar keeping method was probably NOT used in the days of Moses, or for a long while after him. There is nothing to indicate a lunar calendar in any of his Scriptural writings, and if the wilderness Tabernacle faced the east, it was likely to positioned in that manner to determine the equinox for the solar timing of the new year. In addition, Moses linked the calendar to the seasons and harvests, which inherently advocates a solar-based calendar year.

CHAPTER 7

THE ROLE OF THE BABYLONIAN EXILE

Now our research became more focused on historical documentation. We were about to find that data regarding the calendar used by the Babylonian culture during the exile was to become a pivotal aspect.

Israel's Exile and Babylonian Customs

We are finding that the period of the Babylonian exile is likely when the transition to a lunar-based calendar occurred. Old Testament writings record the 70-year judgment of exile that fell upon Judah from roughly 609 BC - 539 BC:

Ezra 5:12
(12) But after that our fathers had provoked the God of heaven unto wrath, he gave them into the hand of Nebuchadnezzar the king of Babylon, the Chaldean, who destroyed this house, and carried the people away into Babylon.

Jeremiah 29:4-7 & 10
(4) Thus saith the LORD of hosts, the God of Israel, unto all that are carried away captives, whom I have caused to be carried away from Jerusalem unto Babylon;
(5) Build ye houses, and dwell in them; and plant gardens, and eat the fruit of them;
(6) Take ye wives, and beget sons and daughters; and take wives for your sons, and give your daughters to husbands, that they may bear sons and daughters; that ye may be increased there, and not diminished.
(7) And seek the peace of the city whither I have caused you to be carried away captives, and pray unto the LORD for it: for in the peace thereof shall ye have peace.
(10) For thus saith the LORD, That after <u>seventy years</u> be accomplished at Babylon I will visit you, and perform my good word toward you, in causing you to return to this place.

Jeremiah indicated that the children of Israel should acclimate to the Babylonian region where they would live for seventy years. However, this would not have meant to adhere to their heathen belief systems. Unfortunately, the old saying, "When in Rome, do as the Romans do", might apply here. We are gratified as we reflect back on the Biblical accounts of Daniel, Shadrach, Meshach, and Abed-nego. They stood their ground and refused to bow to the ways of their captors. Even threat of death could not dissuade them. However, the rest of the nation may not have been so resistant to change.

Indeed, Hershel Shanks offers some agreement:

<u>Ancient Israel From Abraham to the Roman Destruction of the Temple, Revised & Expanded</u> - by Hershel Shanks - p. 211 –

We may assume that not all Jews were faithful to the religion of their parents; some may have assimilated into Babylonian culture.

Although our Bibles are somewhat silent about the progression of the Jewish calendar into what it is today, history may help us piece it together. The Jewish Encyclopedia verifies that the Babylonian calendar year was a soli-lunar system with 354 days:

The 1906 Jewish Encyclopedia - Jewish Encyclopedia.com (the unedited full text of the 1906 Jewish Encyclopedia) -
http://www.jewishencyclopedia.com/articles/3920-calendar-history-of -
The Babylonian years were soli-lunar; that is to say, the year of 12 months containing 354 days was bound to the solar year of 365 days by intercalating, as occasion required, a thirteenth month. Out of every 11 years there were 7 with 12 months and 4 with 13 months. ... The Talmud ... correctly states that the Jews got the names of the months at the time of the Babylonian exile.

A Greek astronomer and mathematician named Meton lived during the time of the Jews' captivity in Babylon. He developed the Metonic cycles which are used in today's Jewish calendars. It is believed that he developed them from the Babylonian culture since they were the influential and supreme world power of that time. The Metonic cycles are a prominent feature of the lunar-based Hillel calendar that was formulated by Hillel II. The Babylonian influence may have been carried down through the Hillel Dynasty due the roots of the dynasty – the Babylonian birth and initial education of Hillel the Elder before he studied later in Jerusalem. It is certainly notable that the Hillel calendar is formed in the same manner as the Babylonian year shown above, AND that it is branded with the names of the Babylonian months!

How Did the Priesthood and its Calendar System Evolve?

One man found favor with Yahweh for his zealous actions to atone for the children of Israel (Numbers 25:7-8). As a result, the covenant of an "everlasting priesthood" was promised to him and to "his seed after him":

Numbers 25:11-13
(11) **Phinehas**, the son of Eleazar, the son of Aaron the priest, hath turned my wrath away from the children of Israel, while he was zealous for my sake among them, that I consumed not the children of Israel in my jealousy.
(12) Wherefore say, Behold, I give unto him my covenant of peace:
(13) And he **shall have it**, **and his seed after him**, even the covenant of **an everlasting priesthood**; because he was zealous for his God, and made an atonement for the children of Israel.

The Holman Bible Dictionary lists the High Priests and their succession, pulling together the Biblical evidence that Zadok was in the line of High Priests that descended from Phinehas (in the line of "his seed after him"). Zadok and all from his lineage who served as priests after him would then be an extension of this line of Phinehas as "his seed after him". Zadok and his descendants would therefore be of the line that would inherit Yahweh's promise of the "everlasting priesthood".

Zadok had a rather prestigious background, as he is credited with anointing Solomon as king (1 Kings 1:32-34). He served for a time as a co-regent priest of sorts with Abiathar. Then after Abiathar was exiled (1 Kings 2:27-35), Zadok was the priest.

1 Kings 2:35

(35) And the king put Benaiah the son of Jehoiada in his room over the host: and Zadok the priest did the king put in the room of Abiathar.

The priesthood of the Zadokite lineage continued, and even presided for a time after Judah's return from Babylon. However, this changed following the campaigns of Alexander the Great. Hellenization was rampant, attitudes were raw and mixed. Tensions flared. Then the Maccabees revolted about 167 to 160 BC, and usurped control. This eventually led to a change in the priesthood as well. The Maccabees ordained their own version of priest (the Hasmoneans), and the Zadokite priesthood was politically and governmentally ended.

The comprehensive online Jewish encyclopedia named Jewish Virtual Library states:

Jewish Virtual Library - Zadok - https://www.jewishvirtuallibrary.org/jsource/judaica/ejud_0002_0021_0_21361.html -
In the Second Temple period, the House of Zadok retained the high priesthood continuously until the Hasmonean revolt.

This same Jewish encyclopedia relates how this priesthood continued through the First Temple period and into the Second. Paraphrasing their findings, the list of high priests in Nehemiah 12 shows the Zadok lineage continuing in the priesthood down through Jaddua in the time of Darius II about 400 BC. The famous historian Josephus then confirms that the Zadokite lineage continued down through Onias III who was the high priest when Antiochus Epiphanes began to rule in 175 BC. Dead Sea Scroll researcher Hershel Shanks then shows us the transition away from the Zadokite line:

Understanding the Dead Sea Scrolls: A Reader From the Biblical Archaeology Review - by Hershel Shanks
– p. 80 -
Then in 172 B.C., Onias III, the legitimate High Priest, was murdered in Jerusalem: Onias was a Zadokite, a priest who was descended from Zadok (King David's high priest and originator of the line of High Priests of the Temple in Jerusalem). In Onias' stead, the Syrian overlords appointed Meneleus, a highly Hellenized Jew who was not of the Zadokite line. To many of the faithful, Meneleus could only be a usurper.

With this shift in power, the Zadokite priesthood vanished from the Temple presence, purportedly withdrawing to the desert regions. This era was one of tremendous transition. There was an intense attempt to force the Greek customs upon the Jewish people, which is known historically as Hellenism. The Second Book of Maccabees is an apocryphal writing that presents the Maccabean uprising that began in 167 BC as a subversive reaction to this Hellenistic effort. The Maccabean revolt resulted in a change of power. This ultimately resulted in a change of the priesthood as well. The Maccabees ordained their own version of priest, known as the Hasmoneans. Unfortunately, this line too was entrenched by Hellenization, and did not retain the pure intents of the Zadokite line. Perhaps for this reason, further judgment followed.

In a presentation of the problems of this day, Hershel Shanks continues:

Understanding the Dead Sea Scrolls: A Reader From the Biblical Archaeology Review - by Hershel Shanks
– p. 80 -
Under the brilliant military leadership of Judas Maccabeus, the revolt was successful, and an independent Jewish state was once again established. ... As matters turned out, however, the Hasmoneans brought not a return to orthodoxy but increased Hellenization. Even Judas himself signed a treaty of friendship with the Roman Senate and employed partly Hellenized Jews as his ambassadors. Finally, in 152 BC, Jonathan had

himself appointed High Priest – another usurpation; for many Jews this act was a great provocation and the strongest reason for abhorring the Hasmoneans.

The Hasmonean priesthood was not a lengthy one. The Romans were about to make a change of authority. Hyrcanus was the last reported Hasmonean ruler. Herod felt threatened, so he had Hyrcanus executed in 30 BC. The Hasmonean priestly rule ended, and the rights of the Jews to govern themselves shifted a bit with the power surge of the new Roman authority. However, the desire for independence remained alive in the hearts of the Jewish people, and other forms of the priesthood persevered.

CHAPTER 8

THE SADDUCEES, THE PHARISEES, AND THE WHO?

Along with studying the Babylonian captivity, we found that we needed to understand a little more fully the emergence of religious/political entities following the return to Israel. Historical sources indicate that considerable power struggles ensued among these groups as Israel endeavored to reform.

Who Were the Essenes?

The Jewish Virtual Library tells us that three principal Jewish sects emerged during the Hasmonean Dynasty. This would have been somewhere in the vicinity of 142-63 B.C. These three sects were the Sadducees, the Pharisees, and the Essenes.

The Sadducees advanced in the priestly role. They were strict adherents to the written law, and they rejected anything that was not written within that law, such as the "oral Law".

The Pharisees believed Moses had been given an "oral Law" which governed the use of the Torah. They recorded principles from this "oral Law" in the book known today as the Talmud. The Pharisees were known as experts in all matters of Jewish law. Their roles were mostly scribal and rabbinic.

The third group was the Essenes. Compiling an extensive number of sources, we find a consensus that they probably splintered off from the Sadducees, abandoning their ranks to render their allegiance to the Zadokite priestly line. Apparently, they took issue with the way the Temple was run, believing that it had been corrupted and defiled after the Zadokite priesthood had departed. The Dead Sea Scrolls speak of the Essenes, and indicate that they adhered to Zadokite teachings, particularly to the instruction of the man they called the "Teacher of Righteousness".

Quoting again from the words of Hershel Shanks relative to the Essenes, we get a glimpse of this Teacher of Righteousness:

Understanding the Dead Sea Scrolls: A Reader From the Biblical Archaeology Review - by Hershel Shanks – p. 80-81 -
Jews disgusted with what they believed to be the pollution of their ancestral religion and revolted by the usurpation of the High Priesthood by non-Zadokites, rallied behind a man they called Moreh Tzedek, the Teacher of Righteousness. No doubt the Teacher of Righteousness was of the Zadokite line, a legitimate claimant to the title of High Priest. He was opposed, however by the Wicked Priest who ruled illegitimately in Jerusalem.

*The faithful retreated to the desert to live a life of ritual purity, observing the ancient law, **following the old calendar that marked the holy times**, and awaiting the day when the Teacher of Righteousness would be* *accepted by all Jews as High Priest and would return once again to Jerusalem.*

Hershel Shanks explains that there are two theories relative to the <u>origin</u> of the Essenes. The first, the Palestinian origin theory, is what we have drawn from so far in quotes from his detailed work in <u>Understanding the Dead Sea Scrolls: ...</u> . The second is known as the Babylonia origin theory, and asserts that the Essenes extend back to the destruction of the first Temple in 586 B.C. About this theory, he states:

<u>Understanding the Dead Sea Scrolls: A Reader From the Biblical Archaeology Review</u> - by Hershel Shanks – p. 81 -
*Many of these Jews, deported from their Judean homeland, perceived the Babylonian Exile as divine punishment. As an appropriately submissive response to this divine judgment, they bound themselves as a group to a perfect observance of the law, determined that history should not repeat itself. Some of this group – whom we may call Essenes – <u>returned to Palestine</u> at what they must have regarded as a propitious moment, the victory of Judas Maccabeus and the renewal of an independent Jewish state. Once there, however, they were bitterly disappointed by the Hellenized forms of Judaism that controlled the state. After an initial attempt to bring their erring brethren to the truth, they retreated to the isolation of Qumran, near the northern end of the Dead Sea. **<u>Led by the Teacher of Righteousness, the Essenes believed that adherence to their precepts was the one sure refuge against the coming messianic judgment</u>**.*

We would emphasize that the "origin" of the Essenes is the question that is debated here. What does seem to be obvious though, is that whatever the origin of the Essene people was, they ultimately became committed to the purity associated with the Zadokite priestly line. Likewise, they adhered to teachings fostered by that lineage through the Moreh Tzedek or Teacher of Righteousness.

Though the Sadducees and the Pharisees did not agree in many respects, these two groups managed to cooperate with one another to run the Temple in their day. They worked together with the elders (the heads of the various Hebrew tribes), forming the Sanhedrin of the second Temple period. The Encyclopedia Britannica confirms that this Sanhedrin made all calendar decisions in Jerusalem at that time. We would recall here that Hillel the Elder presided over the Sanhedrin of his day, followed later by Hillel II. The calendar decisions they made then would have been based on lunar criterion, and loosely hinged to the evolving calendar we know as the Jewish Hillel calendar today. However, the Dead Sea Scrolls and encyclopedic research confirm that some sectarian groups observed a calendar other than the one sanctioned by the Sanhedrin:

<u>Understanding the Dead Sea Scrolls: A Reader From the Biblical Archaeology Review</u> - by Hershel Shanks – p. 81 -
*The faithful retreated to the desert to live a life of ritual purity, observing the ancient law, **<u>following the old calendar that marked the holy times</u>**, ...*

The Essenes were "the faithful" of this passage, so they were the ones who were "following the <u>old calendar</u> that marked the <u>holy times</u>". The aspect we do not want to leave unnoticed here is that this was an "old" calendar, and that the "holy times" this calendar marked would be Father's holy feast days. It had been in use prior to the one that the new priesthood put into effect. It is even possible that the word "old" here meant <u>very</u> old! We will work more with this soon. At the very least, this points to the calendar as being a prime issue that led to the departure of the Zadokite priesthood and the Essenes.

Hershel Shanks is not only a highly-acclaimed author, but he is also the founder and editor of The Biblical Archaeology Society. The vast works of this man brings to the forefront a great deal of information from the numerous Dead Sea Scroll writings. Among these writings is the Temple Scroll. Relative to this scroll, he states:

<u>The Dead Sea Scrolls – Discovery and Meaning</u> – by Hershel Shanks – p. 28 -
The Temple Scroll is sectarian, that is, it belongs to the Dead Sea sect, identified by most scholars with the Essenes. ... <u>The members of the sect did not participate in the cult of the Temple that existed in their period because they regarded it as unclean.</u> ... According to the scroll, <u>the sect had a calendar of its own that was different from the calendar of the rest of the Jewish people.</u>

He amplifies this stance a bit when he states:

<u>The Dead Sea Scrolls – Discovery and Meaning</u> - by Hershel Shanks – p. 22 -
...they had a different calendar than the Jewish authorities who controlled the Temple. This indicates that in some ways the ancient Jewish groups were more diverse than modern Jewish movements, where we have Orthodox, Conservative, Reform and Reconstructionist Jews. Imagine a Jewish movement today that didn't even observe Yom Kippur, the Day of Atonement, the holiest day of the Jewish calendar on the same day as other Jews. Well, that's the case with the Dead Sea Scroll community. They had their own calendar, and <u>they observed the holidays according to that calendar.</u>

The realization that the Essenes viewed the Temple practices during the Hasmonean period as unclean makes perfect sense if they viewed the calendar practices of that priesthood as replacing the <u>clean</u> (what they believed to be Yahweh's instructions) with the <u>unclean</u> (practices adopted from the heathen Babylonian people). Coupled with the fact that the current priesthood was not of the covenanted priestly seed line, this could all work together as their rationale for deeming the current priesthood itself as being "unclean", and for turning their back on it.

Mikhael Bauer of Netzari Virtual Yahadim authored an extensive article titled <u>The Jubilee Calendar: A Major Point of Contention between the Zadokite Priesthood and the Hasmonean Priesthood?</u>. In it he references English archaeologist and Dead Sea Scrolls scholar John M. Allegro, saying that **the Zaddikim (sons of Zadok) taught the solar Jubilee calendar,** <u>which Israel observed until the exile.</u>

Because it is referenced over and again that the Zadokite priesthood preserved the "old" calendar, we have coined the name **<u>Zadokite calendar</u>** for the method of calendar keeping spelled out in the Dead Sea Scroll documents, particularly in <u>The Book of Jubilees.</u>

CHAPTER 9

THE OLD CALENDAR

So, historical references validate that there was an OLD CALENDAR! Wow! Our attention was riveted. If it was this calendar that was in use prior to the captivity, we wanted to know more about it!

So, What Was this Calendar Like?

The backbone of the Zadokite calendar is an exact 52-week year. This makes a significant difference in the duration of the year and the timing of Father's appointed holy days from that of the lunar-based calendar being practiced today. The people of the Scrolls believed so strongly in their calendar that they clearly distinguished the lunar version as causing a great deal of corruption to Yahweh's order and appointed times. What we are calling the Zadokite calendar is often referred to as the Essene calendar or the Jubilees calendar because the prevailing view is that the Essenes followed it, and it is referenced heavily in The Book of Jubilees that they likely wrote. A portion of The Book of Jubilees manuscript actually states:

The Book of Jubilees 6:36-37 - The Researchers Library of Ancient Texts Volume 1 - by R.H. Charles, Oxford – p. 289 -
*... there will be those who will assuredly make observations of the moon -how (it) disturbs the seasons and comes in from year to year ten days too soon. For this reason the years will come upon them when they will disturb (the order), and <u>make an abominable (day) the day of testimony</u>, and an **<u>unclean day</u>** <u>a feast day</u>, and they will <u>confound all the days,</u> **the holy with the unclean, and the unclean day with the holy**; for they will go wrong as to the months and sabbaths and feasts and jubilees.*

The "day of testimony" they reference is almost certainly the Day of Atonement or Yom Kippur, the most sacred and somber day of the calendar year. If the wrong methodology was used to produce the Temple calendar, then this holiest of days would be observed at the wrong time. It would fall on a day that should be rendered as common, making the common day holy. Conversely, the correct day for this holiest day of Yom Kippur would be treated as a common day instead of observing its holy nature. It would be mixing the holy with the profane, and the clean with the unclean.

They saw this as an abomination of major magnitude, and it appears that they associated it with the contamination and defilement of the entire Temple system. The calendar they used did not condone lunar observation to determine months. Doing so would disrupt seasonal and yearly divisions, putting them at the wrong times, and displacing the proper alignment for Yahweh's feast dates.

Scholars believe that Hosea's ministry was about 770-725 BC. Could it be that his words were prophesied (at least in part) to portend the day when Yahweh's feast dates would be observed at the wrong times?

Hosea 2:11
(11) I will also cause all her mirth to cease, her feast days, her <u>new moons</u>, and her sabbaths, and <u>all her solemn feasts</u>.

We can see how keeping a lunar calendar might displace the feast days when the "chodeshim" are not honored on the right days. However, how would this displace the weekly Sabbaths? This may be where the "lunar Sabbath" that we mentioned before fits in. It appears that a Babylonian custom might have made its way back to Israel in this respect as well.

<u>The 1906 Jewish Encyclopedia</u> - Jewish Encyclopedia.com (the unedited full text of the 1906 Jewish Encyclopedia) -
http://www.jewishencyclopedia.com/articles/14813-week
There is ground ... for the assumption that both among the Babylonians and among the Hebrews the first day of the first week of the month was always reckoned as coincident with the first day of the month.

It might have been prophesied by Hosea long ago. This system dictates that both the month AND the week begin at the new moon. They call the 1st day of the new month "new moon day", then they observe every 7th day thereafter as a Sabbath until the next new moon. Using this system, new moon day will be on the 1st, and Sabbaths will always fall on the 8th, the 15th, the 22nd, and the 29th days of the month. Recall that using this system means that there will no longer be exact seven-day spans between the weekly Sabbath that ends the month and the first Sabbath of the next month. Furthermore, the weekly Sabbaths will occur on various days of the week from one month to the next. The entire structure of even the weekly Sabbaths they observe is lunar-based. It appears that Father was speaking of that as well in this passage, where Sabbaths would also become problematic due to observation of the moon.

"New moons" in this Hosea 2:11 reference is "chodeshim". Could it be that the "chodeshim" they should be observing was the seasonal "chodeshim" instead of some variety of lunar observance which had caused several errant deviations? Could this verse have meant that His people's failure to observe their seasonal transitions, their weekly Sabbaths, and their holy feast days in their proper place would bring judgment? Indeed, Yahweh's judgment allowed the Temple to be destroyed in 70 AD.

The "chodeshim", the Sabbaths, and the solemn feasts were all associated here with "mirth". They were times of celebration. There would be gatherings at these celebrations. This not only concurs with <u>The Book of Jubilees</u> reports, but the same concept carries through in reference to the "new moon" ("chodesh") in Isaiah 66 during the Millennial reign as well.

Isaiah 66:23
(23) And it shall come to pass, that <u>from one new moon to another</u>, and from one sabbath to another, shall <u>all flesh come to worship before me</u>, saith the LORD.

The picture of these seasonal "chodesh" events (which we have come to see as the "new moon" events in this Isaiah passage) will be clarified as we look to <u>The Book of Jubilees</u> to explain the calendar they used. As we continue our research with <u>The Book of Jubilees</u>, it should be noted that it was found in fragments of Hebrew manuscript among the Dead Sea Scrolls (along with portions of our Biblical text) in the mid 1900's and THEN translated into English, long after the King James Version had been published. As a quick reminder, the term "new moon(s)" in these manuscripts was almost certainly "chodesh(im)" as well, and it should never have been translated as "new moon" in the scroll translations either. This becomes clear as the full reading of the document reveals a stark and zealous warning AGAINST using the observation of the moon to begin the month. The translation might well have been drawn directly from the King James Bible, and may actually lend credence to the concept that this identical translation issue in our Biblical text was inappropriate as well.

It is very significant that throughout The Book of Jubilees, the use of "chodesh(im)" [translated "new moon(s)"] was typically used in reference to the 1st, 3rd, 4th, 7th, and 10th months. The "chodesh" cyclical transition for these months would be significant because they were times of celebration for the 4 seasonal transitions.

The Book of Jubilees 6:23 - The Researchers Library of Ancient Texts Volume 1 by R.H. Charles, Oxford – p. 288 –
And on the new moon of the first month, and on the new moon of the fourth month, and on the new moon of the seventh month, and on the new moon of the tenth month are the days of remembrance, and the days of the seasons in the four divisions of the year. These are written and ordained as a testimony for ever.

Could the true meaning of the seasonal markers celebrated in these "chodesh" events have been obscured by our translators? Might at least some of these "chodesh" events relate powerfully to the agricultural patterning of seedtime and harvest, cold and heat (winter and summer)?

Genesis 8:22
(22) While the earth remaineth, seedtime and harvest, and cold and heat, and summer and winter, and day and night shall not cease.

Some planting of seed occurs in the spring and is harvested in the fall, whereas other planting of seed occurs in the fall and is harvested in the spring. Therefore, seedtime and harvest can be interchangeable, but point to the spring and fall seasons. These are designated by the equinox markers Yahweh placed in His heavens above for our use in discerning time.

The vernal equinox marks the beginning of seedtime/harvest (spring), the summer solstice marks the beginning of heat (summer), the autumnal equinox marks the beginning of harvest/seedtime (fall), and the winter solstice marks the beginning of cold (winter). They were "chodeshim" – each one being the conclusion of one cycle, and the beginning of the next.

You will recall that in our etymology of "chodesh", we saw the cyclical effect, the beginning of the cycle, going through the door, and the conclusion of the cycle. The cycle can relate to a number of different things. It is not always the same cycle. The changing of the seasons is indeed a type of "chodesh". Once we step away from our Western manner of linear thinking and into the Hebraic cyclical thinking we can see Yahweh's patterning of repeating cycles and cycles within more cycles - it's truly astounding!

A study of Philo seems to correlate. He clearly attributes the beginning of the year in the days of Moses to the time frame of the vernal equinox, and he then links this timing to the dispensation of natural seasonal growth of the crops:

Early Jewish Writings - A Treatise on the Life of Moses, that is to say, On the Theology and Prophetic Office of Moses - Book II - XLI 222 - http://www.earlyjewishwritings.com/text/philo/book25.html -
(222) Moses puts down the beginning of the vernal equinox as the first month of the year, attributing the chief honour, not as some persons do to the periodical revolutions of the year in regard of time, but rather to the

31

graces and beauties of nature which it has caused to shine upon men; for it is through the bounty of nature that the seeds which are sown to produce the necessary food of mankind are brought to perfection. And the fruit of trees in their prime, which is second in importance only to the necessary crops, is engendered by the same power, and as being second in importance it also ripens late; for we always find in nature that those things which are not very necessary are second to those which are indispensable.

Rather than using the availability of crops to determine Yahweh's calendar timing, Moses apparently used Yahweh's celestial timing to start his year, knowing that the crops WOULD BE READY at the appropriate time by using this system. Indeed, the sun WILL follow its subscribed course after this equinox, and the appropriate light and heat from its rays WILL ensure that the barley will be ripened in due course on the Zadokite calendar! Father's planning is always perfect!

Likewise, Philo <u>affixed</u> the Feast of Tabernacles to the time-frame of the Autumnal Equinox:

<u>Early Jewish Writings</u> - <u>The Tenth Festival</u> XXXIII (204) - http://www.earlyjewishwritings.com/text/philo/book28.html -
The last of all the annual festivals is that which is called the <u>feast of tabernacles, which is fixed</u> for <u>the season of the autumnal equinox</u>. And by this festival the lawgiver teaches two lessons, both that it is necessary to honour equality, the first principle and beginning of justice, the principle akin to unshadowed light; and that it is becoming also, after witnessing the perfection of all the fruits of the year, to give thanks to that Being who has made them perfect.

As mentioned above, Isaiah tells of the times in the Millennial reign when people will gather to worship at the Temple:

Isaiah 66:23
(23) And it shall come to pass, that from one new moon to another, and from one sabbath to another, shall all flesh come to worship before me, saith the LORD.

Why would Isaiah not have mentioned Yahweh's feast days in this verse? Could it be that they were actually accounted here to be a part of the "chodesh" that was translated "new moon"? Might one "chodesh" to another include all of the festivities for Yahweh's seasonal markers and His specific holy days? From one "chodesh" to another, and from one Sabbath to another are the two primary focal points of the Zadokite calendar which chronicles the various holy days (including seasonal transitions) that were celebrated by Father's people.

The Book of Jubilees

Though <u>The Book of Jubilees</u> is not a part of the Scriptural canon commonly acknowledged today, there are some Christians who revere it as canon. Referring to <u>The Book of Jubilees</u>, the New World Encyclopedia says:

<u>New World Encyclopedia</u> - Jubilees, Book of - http://www.newworldencyclopedia.org/entry/Jubilees,_Book_of –
*... sometimes called the <u>Lesser Genesis</u>... **it is still considered canonical for the Ethiopian Orthodox Church ...**

Indeed, it does not appear that there are any conflicts between its text and the Scriptures we revere as canon today. It actually provides additional details that are missing in our Biblical text, filling in more names in the genealogies, and routinely including the names of the wives and daughters. It can also be instrumental in leading to a fuller understanding of the Hebrew term "chodesh".

While there are ample indications regarding the celebration of "chodesh" events, specific information is missing there too. Since The Book of Jubilees does not go into detail about these memorial celebrations, the exact beginning and conclusion of them is difficult to pinpoint. There are, however, whispers in some writings that allude to these celebrations of Yahweh's seasonal transitions being 3-day festivals. This does make some sense. The Zadokite calendar inserts an intercalary day at the conclusion of each 90-day quarter. The placement of these intercalary days is spelled out in The Book of Jubilees. The celebration might well begin on the last day of the quarter, continue through the intercalary day to complete the seasonal cycle, then conclude after the 1st day of the new cycle. The celebration would then see out the old, make the transition, and bring in the new.

In 1 Samuel, we see the inference that the "new moon" ("chodesh") might have been a 3-day event.

1 Samuel 20:5 & 19
(5) And David said unto Jonathan, Behold, to morrow is the new moon, and I should not fail to sit with the king at meat: but let me go, that I may hide myself in the field unto the third day at even.
(19) And **when thou hast stayed three days**, then thou shalt go down quickly, and come to the place where thou didst hide thyself when the business was in hand, and shalt remain by the stone Ezel.

The "third day" and "three days" of what? Why was this 3-day period significant? Could the "third day" wording of verse 5 have been implying the 3rd day of the "chodesh" celebration? Might not David have then indicated that Jonathan was to come to him "when thou hast stayed three days", or concluded the celebration?

1 Samuel 20:27
(27) And it came to pass on the morrow, which was the second day of the month, that David's place was empty: and Saul said unto Jonathan his son, Wherefore cometh not the son of Jesse to meat, neither yesterday, nor to day?

The word "month" in this verse is "chodesh". The 2nd day of this event is still referenced as "chodesh" though the month is no longer "new". This would certainly indicate that "chodesh" is an extended event rather than simply a day to start the month. This could easily be inferring the 2nd day of the 3-day seasonal transition celebration.

Let's look again at the words of Lawrence Schiffman:

Reclaiming the Dead Sea Scrolls - by Lawrence H. Schiffman - p. 292 -
When the seasons begin on the days of the New Moon,
when together at their end they succeed one another. ...

Presuming the word for "New Moon" is "chodesh", it could actually be saying that the seasons begin during the extended "chodesh" event (on the "days" of [plural]), or during the transition from one cycle to the next. These cycles then continue in the pattern ordained by Yahweh, as "together at their end they succeed one another". This would be the 3-day transition from the old cycle to the new, and the continuing cyclical pattern throughout the year.

In 1 Samuel, the timing for "chodesh" is known in advance of its arrival, as though it had been spelled out in the layout of a congruent calendar system where celebration events had been predetermined. These 3 days of its celebration might be very important. As we have suggested, the "second" day of "chodesh" might mean the 2nd day of the "chodesh" event rather than the 2nd day of the new month. Jonathan was to remain with Saul for the entire 3 days and then go to meet with David. David would remain hidden until the "third day at even", or the conclusion of the 3rd day. It was a time when gathering together was expected, as verse 5 says "I should not fail to sit with the king at meat", and in verse 27, "Wherefore cometh not the son of Jesse to meat, neither yesterday, nor to day?"

Since the timing of this event is thought to have occurred almost 900 years prior to the emergence of the Hasmonean priesthood, it would have preceded the corruption of the priesthood and the resulting Babylonian influence on the Temple calendar system. Might the Hebrew people in David's day have been observing "the **old** calendar" at that time, a calendar that actually honored the cyclical patterning presented in The Book of Jubilees – a calendar that celebrated the seasonal transitions as they were presented in these scroll documents?

CHAPTER 10

LUNI-SOLAR – OR NOT?

We were now seeing a distinct departure from the lunar-based calendar system, and the emergence of a solar-based system. It had almost seemed absurd to us, yet we couldn't refute what we were seeing. This was a drastic change from the status quo, but if what was coming into view was really God's calendar system, we couldn't turn away from it. We had hoped we could disprove it, but the reality of it was becoming more evident with each step we took. We aren't big fans of change, and we surely didn't want to make waves in the fellowships we cherished, but these considerations could not stand up against the evidence that kept coming our way. We hadn't given up the fight yet though. We would keep trying to find a disqualifying factor, starting by looking into the way this calendar functioned. We would then turn over every stone of historical documentation we could, while maintaining at all times the strict filter of Truth contained only within Biblical Scripture.

Using the Zadokite Calendar

Using simplified analogies, the equinox in the spring and again in the fall occurs when the days and nights are of equal length. Therefore, the amount of the sun's light during these 24-hour periods is the determining factor of the equinox markers. In that sense, the Zadokite calendar is a solar-based system. Likewise, the duration of the year on this calendar equates closely to the actual duration of the solar year. Conversely, most years on today's lunar-based calendar systems are 10 days shorter than the actual solar year, but they can be about a month longer in others. That is what is meant in verse 36 of The Book of Jubilees text when it says that observation of the moon will make the next year come ten days too soon:

The Book of Jubilees 6:36 - The Researchers Library of Ancient Texts Volume 1 - by R.H. Charles, Oxford – p. 289 -
... *there will be those who will assuredly make observations of the moon -how (it) disturbs the seasons and comes in from year to year ten days too soon.*

The Essenes demonstrate a strong affiliation to Genesis 1:14 regarding the signs given by Father in the sky above us, and they use only these signs to distinguish one year from the next. They realize that the sun, moon, and stars were put in the sky as timekeeping mechanisms. It is for that reason that they start their year on the day of the week when Father put these lights in the sky for us.

Josephus likewise speaks of the 4th day of creation when he says:

The Works of Josephus Complete and Unabridged - Translated by William Whiston, A.M. - Antiquities of the Jews - 1.1.1 – p. 29 -
*On the fourth day he adorned the heaven with the sun, the moon, and the other stars; and **appointed them their motions and courses**, that the vicissitudes of the seasons might be clearly signified.*

The Biblical Calendar Then and Now

Vicissitudes simply means "changes". The motions and courses of the sun through the stars brings varying amounts of light to the earth. This determines the equinoxes and solstices, which in turn determine the changes ("vicissitudes") of the season. This then distinctly indicates the 4 markers of the equinoxes and the solstices which determine the onset for the changes in the seasons. The day God put the lights in our sky was day 4 of the creation week, so timekeeping wasn't possible until that day. Once these lights in the sky had been put in place, the tracking of time began. Because the Zadokite year always makes a complete circuit, the new year always begins on a weekday 4 - the 1st weekday 4 (Wednesday) after the vernal (spring) equinox.

The standard Zadokite calendar year is an even 364-day year. There are 4 quarters, which correspond to the equinox and solstice markers. The year goes from the vernal (spring) equinox to the summer solstice, the summer solstice to the autumnal (fall) equinox, the autumnal equinox to the winter solstice, and the winter solstice back to the vernal equinox and the start of the next year. Because the years always start on a weekday 4 (Wednesday), there are always even weeks in the year. A year of 364 days is 52 weeks of 7 days each.

The 4 quarters are each divided into 3 months, making 12 months in the year. The months are 30 days each, with an extra intercalary day being added at the end of each 3-month period as a marker between the seasons. For the sake of simplicity, the calendar reflects this intercalary day as a 31st day at the end of every 3 months. It depicts the 1st and 2nd month of each quarter as being 30 days, and the 3rd month as being 31 days. This makes 91 days in each quarter and 364 days in the average year. There is never a 13th month added. This is a trait worth noting, as neither does the Bible ever mention such a thing as a 13th month. Even the priestly duties were assigned based on 24 courses to span the 12-month year. There were no extra courses to cover a 13th month.

These 12 months correspond to the 12 houses in Yahweh's Mazzaroth. The changing of the month correlates well to the astronomical entrance of the sun into a new Mazzaroth house. The sun and the stars work in tandem in this calendar system.

Likewise, maybe there is never a Biblical inference of a 29-day month because Yahweh never intended that the duration of the lunar cycle should be used to determine the length of a month. As previously mentioned, the Bible seems to routinely reckon the length of a month to be 30 days.

Putting together what we have seen so far, let's look again at Psalm 81. We will refresh it here for your reference:

Psalms 81:3
(3) Blow up the trumpet in the new moon, in the time appointed, on our solemn feast day.

Let's dissect it carefully to see what it might really be saying.

The single Hebrew word for the phrase "blow up" is Strong's H8628 (taqa`) - *to blow, clap, strike, sound, thrust, give a blow, blast.*

The Hebrew word for trumpet is Strong's H7782 (showphar) - *horn, ram's horn.*

The single Hebrew word for the phrase "solemn feast day" is Strong's H2282 - chag - *festival, feast, festival-gathering, pilgrim-fest, feast, festival sacrifice.*

The single Hebrew word for the phrase "time appointed" is Strong's H3677 (kece') - *full moon, fullness of a time*

We would note that in the typical "new moon" scenario of the lunar calendar, the "full moon" aspect for "time appointed" has been troubling to many of us. We couldn't see how the "new moon" and the "full moon" could both apply here. Maybe they don't. Let's put it together with the Zadokite calendar in mind. Recall now that "chodesh" can simply mean the transition of the closing of any non-specific cycle and the start of another. Bearing this in mind maybe the following would make perfect sense.

"Blow" the "shofar" at the "seasonal transitions" in the "fullness of the completed cycle" on our "festival gathering".

If indeed those who kept the Zadokite calendar understood the festival nature of the equinox and solstice markers, and observed these celestial signs of Yahweh with gatherings, this could explain the verse well. It could also explain all of the other gatherings, celebrations, etc. that are associated with the various English references to "new moon" throughout the Old Testament.

Let's reference a verse in Numbers at this time:

Numbers 10:10
(10) Also in the day of your gladness, and <u>in your solemn days</u>, **and** <u>in the beginnings of your months, ye shall blow with the trumpets over your burnt offerings</u>, and over the sacrifices of your peace offerings; that they may be to you for a memorial before your God: I am the LORD your God.

The word "months" here is also a version of "chodeshim", with the letter "kaph" inserted in the plural suffix to show possession (your). Here again is the blowing of the trumpet during Yahweh's solemn feast days AND in the beginnings of the "chodeshim", which might mean the beginning of their seasons, though it could very well mean their months (30-day intervals) as well. Again though, there is no reference to the moon here at all.

The Hebrew word for "beginnings" is Strong's H7218 (ro'sh) - *head, top, summit, upper part, chief, total, sum, height, front, beginning*. Note that it means "beginning", but also "total, sum". We therefore see the implication of a completed cycle here as well as the start of a new one.

Therefore, we see that blowing the trumpet in the times of gladness can include a number of things - celebrations of a number of transitional cycles ("chodeshim").

There are no month or day names in this "old" 364-day calendar. There is no indication of any Babylonian influence whatsoever within it as it was recorded in the Dead Sea Scrolls. The Babylonian month names are exclusive to the lunar-based calendar adapted by the Sanhedrin after the exile, and the various lunar-based calendars derived from its roots by others today. All months and days of the Zadokite calendar are simply numbered. Often Roman numerals designate the month, and our Arabic numerals follow the month with the dating of the day. For instance, III-15 would be the 3rd month, the 15th day. Even the days of the week are numbered, as in weekday 1, weekday 2 or weekday 3 for any given week, instead of Sunday, Monday, or Tuesday, etc. (which are associated with the names of other gods).

Exodus 23:13
(13) And in all things that I have said unto you be circumspect: and make no mention of the name of other

gods, neither let it be heard out of thy mouth.

Therefore, I-1 is the 1st day of the 1st month - the beginning day of the new year. It is always placed on the 1st weekday 4 (Wednesday) after the vernal equinox. From there, the rest of the calendar simply falls into place until the next vernal equinox. It is really that simple! Regarding the precise details of the year's transition, the Hebrew day begins in the evening, so it appears that sundown Jerusalem time on weekday 4 (Wednesday) is the determining factor. If the equinox falls before sundown on the weekday 4 (Wednesday) at the end of the yearly cycle, the year starts that same day. If the equinox is after sundown on a weekday 4 (Wednesday), the new year starts the following week on weekday 4 (Wednesday). That means that an extra week (or additional 7 days out of time) will be needed before starting the new year. This happens every 6 years or so. This extra week instead of an extra month makes the calendar much more stable, and 1 week is the most that would ever need to be added. Even then though, the year is composed of exact weeks, being 53 weeks instead of 52.

This demonstrates why this calendar is also referred to as the Sabbath calendar. The Zadokite 364-day calendar puts the emphasis of the calendar on the weekly Sabbath rather than on the month. There are some distinct advantages to this weekly anchor. This anchor assures that the festivals always fall on the same day of the week each year.

There is no need for postponements (adjusting the start of a month so the dating of Holy days does not conflict with Sabbaths, etc.). Each of Yahweh's holy days is firmly affixed to a specific weekday, and this NEVER fluctuates. The fast of the Day of Atonement is on a weekday 6 each year, and it is broken by the celebration and feasting of the weekly Sabbath. The flow is fabulous!

CHAPTER 11

FATHER'S TREMENDOUS PATTERNING

How could we ignore the patterns we were about to see? They were to be amazing! But, we're jumping ahead. We'll share them with you now!

Calendar Patterns

Deuteronomy 5:13-14
(13) Six days thou shalt labour, and do all thy work:
(14) But the seventh day is the sabbath of the LORD thy God: …

Our understanding regarding the weekly Sabbath is pretty simple: Yahweh's Word seems abundantly clear here that His weekly Sabbath is static. It is unalterable and never changes. It is consistently 7 days from the preceding weekly Sabbath. It is 6 days of work, followed by 1 of rest, then the repeat of the same over and again. It was designed after the week of creation in which Yahweh worked 6 days, then rested on the 7th. There is no deviation there whatsoever. Exodus 31:16 tells us that this is a perpetual pattern, and perpetual means: *lasting forever, never-ending*. When there are intervening holy days of rest during the 6 working days of the week, the "rest" aspect overrides the "work" for those specific days. Even then though, the flow and count from the preceding weekly Sabbath to the following one is uninterrupted. Even Yahweh's SPECIAL intervening holy days do not disrupt the continual and perpetual count of 7 – it marches on unaltered.

The weekly Sabbath is simply NOT affixed in any way to any celestial display. It is not affected in the least by the equinox (which is determined by Earth's position relative to the sun), or by the sun itself, or by the moon, or by the stars. The DAYS themselves are marked by the appearance of the sun and moon, but the weeks are determined by the counting of 7's. The only thing the weekly Sabbath is linked to is the weekly Sabbath before it, and a count of 7. As long as days and nights continue, that count is never to be interrupted or altered in any way.

Yahweh provides a Heavenly display to show us specifically certain aspects of space and time:

Genesis 1:14
(14) And God said, Let there be lights in the firmament of the heaven to divide the day from the night; and let them be **for signs**, and **for seasons**, and **for days**, and **years**:

The word "signs" here is the Hebrew word Strong's H226 ('owth) – *sign, marker, signal, banner, token, ensign, standard.*

Being side by side in the same verse, Yahweh then indicates that discernment of these Heavenly time-keeping lights and signs apply to 3 and only 3 aspects of time: **seasons**, **days**, and **years**. The lights of His majestic handiwork, and His markers, ensigns, banners, standards and tokens are what our Father put in place in the Heavens to signal the start and conclusion of <u>these 3 specific</u> periods of time. To add to Yahweh's list of 3 in this verse, is to add to His Word with that which may not have been intended by it at all! The sun and moon show us the start and end of the light and darkness that form our **days**. The equinoxes and solstices (as determined by the sun) are the signs (markers, ensigns or banners) Father provides to signal the start and end of each of the 4 **seasons**, and His stars provide the backdrop to these markers to validate them. Likewise, the spring equinox (as determined by the sun) is the specific marker that signals the start and end of our **years**, and it is confirmed by the stars as well. Psalms actually seems to indicate that these solstice markers which depend upon the sun's light signify the start of summer and winter:

Psalms 74:16-17
(16) The day is thine, the night also is thine: thou hast prepared the light and the sun.
(17) Thou hast set all the borders of the earth: thou hast made summer and winter.

The Hebrew word for "borders" is Strong's H1367 (gĕbuwlah) – *boundary.* The "borders of the earth" in verse 17 would then be the solstice markers which provide the boundaries and borders for the seasons of summer and winter.

Conversely, there is no valid Biblical evidence whatsoever that our weeks or months are remotely dictated by or calculated from the sun, moon, stars, or signs in the Heavens. Likewise, none of Yahweh's weekly Sabbath days, His annual festival days, His Shemitah (Sabbath for the land) years (Leviticus 25:4), or His Jubilee years (Leviticus 25:11) are determined in that manner. Some would insist that the word "seasons" in Genesis 1:14 is referring to these holy days. The Hebrew word for "seasons" here is Strong's H4150 (mow`ed) – ***an appointed sign or signal, sacred season, an appointed season, an appointed time,*** *an appointed place, appointed meeting, tent of meeting, set feast.* However, in this case, "mowed" may simply mean "seasons". In fact, Father's four seasons might be very sacred to Him, as they provide the rhythmic synthesis of his agricultural and festival cycles. These then compose the spokes of his annual wheel.

As a brief refresher, we will repeat the concept quickly: While "chodesh(im) is sometimes translated as "new moon(s)" in our English Bibles, it seems that the Hebrew etymology actually corresponds more realistically to the equinoxes and solstices (the appointed signs or signals) that begins Yahweh's appointed SEASONS. The Hebrew word for "moon" is actually something else entirely: Strong's H3394 - (yareach). Then when we realize that such appointed "chodesh" times for the seasonal changes were often celebrated with a gathering of Yahweh's people to feast, the true meaning of "mow`ed" comes to light. It is not just one aspect, but the entire spectrum of the definition above that is significant here – sign, signal, season, appointed time, etc. Maybe a little twist has led us astray for far too long!

Indeed, the "chodesh" of the spring equinox IS a very important season, as it is this appointed sign that determines the start of the year from which all other appointed times are counted. The "chodesh" markers for Yahweh's sacred seasonal changes are appointed by Him and conform easily to the counting process. In accordance with Genesis 1:14, Yahweh's timing is performed as follows: The sun and moon continually mark our days. The position of the sun determines the equinox and solstice markers which usher in our 4 seasons, and the spring equinox signals the timing for our new year. The stars in the Heavenly Mazzaroth then confirm the new seasons and the new year. Genesis 1:14 has then basically been completed until it is time for the start of the following new year. The rest of the timing in Yahweh's calendar is simply determined through counting the days that the sun and moon establish.

In reality, all of Father's festival holy days listed in Torah are derived by counting. Father specifies that Passover is on the 14th day of the 1st month and Unleavened Bread is on the 15th day. It runs for 7 days, and the 1st and 7th days of this 7-day period are holy days. First fruits is the morrow after the Sabbath when you reap your harvest. Pentecost (Feast of Weeks) is counted from the waving of the first fruits. The 1st day of the 7th month is Feast of Trumpets, the 10th day of the same month is Day of Atonement, and the 15th day of that month begins Feast of Tabernacles. The 1st and 8th days of Tabernacles are holy days. Every instance involves some degree of counting or numbering from an event, and the events themselves are derived exclusively by counting. He does not specify that the moon or any of its phases in any way determines the beginning of a holy day, or even the start of the month from which the count to the holy day is based. We now perceive that when one carries forward the root understanding of "chodesh", there is absolutely no relevance to the phases of the moon or any other celestial sign to the timing of the week, the month, or Father's feast days. Only our 24-hour days, and the seasonal transitions are signaled by Yahweh's celestial clock, and the year is then established when the spring equinox marker is seen, just as Genesis 1:14 specifies. From there, all else is simply counted.

Counting and Father's Timing Template

It becomes apparent that the heavens are not operative when determining the specific time parameters of the **week** and the **month** because a sacred principle is at work in the "counting" of them. <u>Employing any version of celestial markers to establish the week and month would totally distort the sacred principle that is carried through in these counts.</u> Though this principle of counting days is expounded time and again in the Biblical text, its importance is frequently discounted. No matter how unintentional it might be, when human intellect subverts Yahweh's intent through misinterpretation, all kinds of distortions follow. The perpetual count of 7 is sacred to Father, and we will see that it plays into the entirety of the calendar system in a very meaningful way.

The sacred patterning of Yahweh is not only found in the 7-day week. There are 7 branches of the Menorah; the New Testament records that the number for forgiveness of sins should be 70 X 7; and there is a 7-day consecration period for the priesthood. Likewise, in Revelation there are 7 churches, 7 seals, 7 trumpets, and 7 vials/bowls, as well as multiple mentions of the 7 spirits of God. There are so many references to 7 in the Word that it makes one's head spin.

It is even the count of 7 that will conclude time itself at the end of the 7th "millennial day" of time. There are 7 "millennial days" (seven 1000-year periods) of time presented in the Bible, and the 7th is a "millennial day" (1000-year period) of rest. This is the patterning that the sacred 7-day week of creation foreshadows with its 6 days of work followed by the 7th day of rest. Yahweh has replicated this "week" over and over again so we could begin to grasp the sacred nature of it <u>and</u> the patterning of the number 7 that comprises it. It is His seal of sacred 7's.

The beauty of the Zadokite calendar (Sabbath calendar) is the uniformity of 52 EXACT 7-day weeks, each containing a Sabbath. Likewise, each quarter contains 13 EXACT 7-day weeks, each containing a Sabbath. Let no person deceive you about how important Yahweh's Sabbaths are to Him! This sacredness is derived from His very act of creation in His 7-day week. He actually hallowed the 7th day Sabbath that concluded His week of creation:

Exodus 20:11
(11) For in six days the LORD made heaven and earth, the sea, and all that in them is, and <u>rested the seventh</u>

day: wherefore the LORD blessed the <u>sabbath day, and hallowed it</u>.

The "sacred 7" principle is Father's foundation for time and all that is related to it, and His 7-day week is the framework for His calendar that relates His time to His people!

Even when folks begin to see the need to transition to a solar-based system, there can be problems in putting this sacred principle into its proper perspective. It cannot be structured in just any manner. This calendar is specific. It upholds the sacred seven of God's creative week.

The solar year is 365.242 days long, and the sun determines when the equinox and solstice markers will appear. Therefore, if we affix our calendar criteria to the <u>precise</u> equinox or solstice date, we will have slightly more than 364 days in the year. Rather than being composed of 52 EXACT 7-day weeks, the year will be 52 weeks <u>plus</u> a fractional fragment of another week. Likewise, those who adjust each quarter of the year to the <u>precise</u> equinox or solstice will find that each quarter of the year will no longer be 13 EXACT 7-day weeks. The principle of the sacred 7 will be disrupted on a routine basis in this type of calendar observation. The quarters and the year will be left with fractional weeks, some of which contain Sabbaths, and others which do not, disrupting the Sabbath flow of the calendar.

Below is an excerpt from <u>The Book of Jubilees</u>. Please note as you read this excerpt that this book was originally written in Hebrew, and the English translation of "new moon(s)" was almost assuredly "chodesh(im)" in the Hebrew manuscripts for this book as well. Likely suffering the same fate as our English Bibles, it is probable that the translation of "new moon" in the text of this book is also a poor one. The "chodeshim" of the 1st, 4th, 7th, and 10th months <u>would not be associated with the moon at all</u>, as evidenced later in this same passage where observance of the moon to determine months is soundly condemned. In this excerpt, you will see it clearly stated that not only the duration of the full year, but also that of each of the 4 Seasons was to consist of a specific number of full weeks with no remaining days. As the seasons progressed from the 1st to the 2nd, to the 3rd, and then to the 4th, each season had 13 complete weeks with no leftover days, and the year was never considered to be complete until 52 unbroken weeks were accomplished. We will refresh the text of this passage from <u>The Book of Jubilees</u> for you here:

The Book of Jubilees 6:25-32 - <u>The Researchers Library of Ancient Texts Volume 1</u> - by R.H. Charles, Oxford – p. 288 -

And **on the new moon of the first month** he was bidden to make for himself an ark, and on that (day) the earth became dry and he opened (the ark) and saw the earth. And on the **new moon of the fourth month** the mouths of the depths of the abyss beneath were closed. And on **the new moon of the seventh month** all the mouths of the abysses of the earth were opened, and the waters began to descend into them. And on the **new moon of the tenth month** the tops of the mountains were seen, and Noah was glad. And on this account he ordained them for himself as feasts for a memorial for ever, and thus are they ordained. And <u>they placed them on the heavenly tablets</u>, **each had thirteen weeks**; <u>from one to another</u> (passed) their memorial, <u>from the first to the second, and from the second to the third, and from the third to the fourth</u>. And all the days of the commandment will be **<u>two and fifty weeks</u>** of days, and (these will make) the entire year complete. Thus it is engraven and ordained on the heavenly tablets. And there is no neglecting (this commandment) for a single year or from year to year. And command thou the children of Israel that they observe the years **according to this reckoning- three hundred and sixty-four days, and (these) will constitute a complete year**, and they will not disturb its time from its days and from its feasts; for everything will fall out in them according to their testimony, and they will not leave out any day nor disturb any feasts.

The Book of Jubilees relates repeatedly to counts of 7. That is why The Book of Jubilees specifies that the year be 52 weeks of days, totaling to exactly 364 days. Weeks of days are full 7-day weeks, so 52 X 7 equals the 364 days – never less. We know that the extra week has to happen on occasion to conform to the reality of the exact solar year, but even then, the year is ALWAYS composed of exact "weeks of days" (7-day weeks).

The glue that holds the very fabric of The Book of Jubilees together is the integrity of the Sabbath week being exactly, fully, and always 7 complete days, with no exceptions. The sacred 7 is what has maintained the count of the weeks from the onset of creation throughout time, and it is consistent yet today. The number 7 is critical to the continuity of timekeeping in The Book of Jubilees, an affidavit of how sacred it is to Yahweh Himself. The Book of Jubilees confirms that even the count to the year of Jubilee is merely 7 more sets of 7. In the count to the Jubilee year, each set of 7 years ended in a Shemitah or Sabbath year of REST to the land. Our Bibles tell of these Sabbath years in Leviticus:

Leviticus 25:3-4
(3) Six years thou shalt sow thy field, and six years thou shalt prune thy vineyard, and gather in the fruit thereof;
(4) But in the seventh year shall be a sabbath of rest unto the land, a sabbath for the LORD: thou shalt neither sow thy field, nor prune thy vineyard.

This shows the sacred pattern of 7 from the creation week being carried over into years – for 6 years the land is worked, and the 7th year it rests. There are 7 sets of 7s en route to the Jubilee year, with a Shemitah year to conclude each of these 7 sets. There is no Biblical instruction whatsoever to disrupt this pattern, even when the Jubilee year arrives.

The Jubilee is special in that it really shouts out the sacredness of the weeks. It is built around a 49-year period, 49 being an amplification of the sacred 7 pattern, as it is 7 X 7, a week of weeks. Jubilee is then the year that follows this set of 49 years.

The Bible and The Book of Jubilees informs us that each 50th year (the Jubilee year) is also a type of Sabbath year, making 2 years in a row of rest for the land.

Leviticus 25:11
(11) A jubilee shall that fiftieth year be unto you: ye shall not sow, neither reap that which groweth of itself in it, nor gather the grapes in it of thy vine undressed.

These 2 years would be the 7th year of the 7th set of years (year 49) and the following year (year 50) at the conclusion of the sacred 49-year span. The Book of Jubilees further documents that this 50th year of Jubilee was actually year 1 of the next set of 7 years. Even the Jubilee year did NOT disrupt the continual flow of 7's, which is ALWAYS kept intact. The Jubilee year then does not contradict that patterning, since it also begins the count of seven 7's to the next Jubilee year. While some see a new count of 50 beginning AFTER the 50th year, this would disrupt the flow of 7's, and it simply cannot be without crushing Yahweh's sacred pattern. Let's look deeper.

Yahweh's holy Sabbath annual festival days never disrupt the consecutive count of Yahweh's week by adding extra days to His perpetual count of 7 in the sacred span of His week.

In precisely the same manner, Yahweh's holy Sabbath Shemitah and Jubilee years never disrupt the consecutive count of Yahweh's week of weeks by adding extra years to His perpetual count of 7 in the sacred span of His week of weeks. His celebration <u>after</u> the completion of 7 times 7 years in no way stops His continuous progression of 7's.

Pentecost has 7 weeks of 7 days each which lead to the day of celebration on the 50th day. It is even called the Feast of Weeks. It separates the spring feasts from the fall feasts with a celebration of Yahweh's sacred 7's. Leviticus 23:15-16 verifies that Pentecost is always on the 1st day of the week, directly after the 7th Sabbath of the 49-day count. Since day 49 is a weekly Sabbath day, and day 50 or Pentecost is an Annual Sabbath, this makes 2 Sabbath days of rest in a row. However, this 50th day is still the 1st day of the following week. In other words, the 1st day of the new week is not the day AFTER Pentecost, it is ON Pentecost day. Annual Sabbaths do not disturb weekly Sabbath counts. Likewise, the 1st year of the next 7-year Shemitah count is not the year AFTER Jubilee, it is ON Jubilee year. Yahweh's flow of time is consistent! <u>The 50th day (Pentecost) is the 1st day in the next count of 7 days</u>. <u>The count of 7 to the next Sabbath day (day 7) is not disrupted</u>. The Jubilee year is precisely the same. <u>The 50th year (Jubilee) is the 1st year in the next count of 7 years</u>. <u>The count to the next Shemitah (year 7) is not disrupted</u>. The Jubilee year is a perfect match to its mini-version, Pentecost, the Feast of Weeks.

Yahweh's patterning is quite obvious, and repetitive in many ways. His entire creation is designed with patterns to point us to Him. The dedicated folks at <u>Messianic Prophecy Bible Project</u> at MessianicBible. com send out wonderful news briefs and interesting information almost daily to subscribers. The 01/16/17 publication is about the significance of numbers, and it concurs beautifully with our findings. It says the number 7 "symbolizes perfection in the natural realm and figures prominently in our experience of time". We concur and realize this even more keenly as we see Yahweh's week of creation being concluded with rest and deemed as hallowed or sacred.

Exodus 20:11
(11) For in six days the LORD made heaven and earth, the sea, and all that in them is, and rested the seventh day: wherefore the LORD blessed the sabbath day, and hallowed it.

Likewise, the number 12 is associated with completion. The same publication says of this number that it "symbolizes totality, wholeness, and the completion of Yahweh's purpose. ... The number 12 is also linked to the concept of time; ... They divided the day and the night into 12-hour periods."

There were 12 apostles, 12 stones in the breastplate of the priest, and 12 manner of precious stones and pearls in the 12 gates of the "new Jerusalem". There were 12 manner of fruit in the garden of the coming kingdom, and 12 stars on the woman's head in Revelation 12. There were 12 thousand from each of the 12 tribes to form the 144,000 of Revelation 7, as well as the repeat of this number who are referred to as first fruits redeemed unto Yahweh and the Lamb in Revelation chapter 14. Jacob's lineage was completed through the birth of 12 sons, which were later designated as the 12 tribes. There were 12 significant stones drawn from the River Jordan to symbolize these 12 brothers and their offspring that came from Jacob's loins.

Joshua 4:2-3
(2) Take you <u>twelve men out of the people, out of every tribe a man,</u>
(3) And command ye them, saying, Take you hence out of the midst of Jordan, out of the place where the priests' feet stood firm, <u>twelve stones,</u> and ye shall carry them over with you, and leave them in the lodging place, where ye shall lodge this night.

<u>The Wisdom in the Hebrew Months</u> by Zvi Ryzman, as well as numerous other writings, even draws a one-to-one direct correlation between these 12 months and the 12 tribes. Some would say there are more than 12 tribes listed in the Word since Ephraim and Manasseh are counted as tribes sometimes, and Levi is omitted at times. The interesting thing though is that in spite of this, the Word never lists 13 or 14 tribes in the Word, but <u>only and always just 12</u>, adjusting the list by omitting Levi or even Dan, etc. This in itself speaks conclusively to the sacredness of the number 12 to Father.

There are 7 days in the week, and 12 months in the year. Both of these numbers are highly significant in Father's time-keeping structure. Just as a week is never to have more or less than 7 days, it appears quite evident that a year should never have more or less than 12 months!

CHAPTER 12

CALENDAR PATTERNS EMERGING IN THE TABERNACLE

Then we found an interesting pattern within the Tabernacle itself, specifically in reference to some of the implements. God provided specific instructions for the formation of these implements. Maybe there was a reason for this!

Tabernacle Implements

Leviticus 24 tells of the Menorah with its 7 branches, and the Table of Shewbread with its 12 cakes or loaves. The directions to make the Menorah given in Exodus 25:31-37 stipulate its intricate fabrication. The Bible never fully clarifies why the Menorah was to have 7 branches or the purpose behind the combinations of 7's in the bowls, knops and flowers. Neither does it disclose the meaning behind the 12 cakes or loaves on the Table of Shewbread. The Scriptural text just informs us that the priests were to "order" them "continually".

Leviticus 24:1-8
(1) And the LORD spake unto Moses, saying,
(2) Command the children of Israel, that they bring unto thee pure oil olive beaten for the light, to cause the lamps to burn continually.
(3) Without the vail of the testimony, in the tabernacle of the congregation, shall Aaron order it from the evening unto the morning before the LORD continually: it shall be a statute for ever in your generations.
(4) **He shall <u>order</u> the lamps upon the pure candlestick before the LORD <u>continually</u>.**
(5) And thou shalt take fine flour, and bake twelve cakes thereof: two tenth deals shall be in one cake.
(6) And thou shalt set them in two rows, six on a row, upon the pure table before the LORD.
(7) And thou shalt put pure frankincense upon each row, that it may be on the bread for a memorial, even an offering made by fire unto the LORD.
(8) Every sabbath **he shall set it in <u>order</u> before the LORD <u>continually</u>**, being taken from the children of Israel by an everlasting covenant.

It was the duty of the priests to maintain the calendar for the people and to inform them when the feast days would be. How were they to do this? Let's think about the Menorah and the Table of Shewbread a bit more.

Both the Menorah (verse 4) and the Shewbread (verse 8) were to be **ORDERED before Yahweh CONTINUALLY!** What on earth does this mean? The word "order" is Strong's H6186 (`arak) - *to <u>arrange</u>, <u>set or put or lay in order</u>, <u>set in array</u>, <u>prepare</u>, order, <u>ordain</u>, handle, furnish, esteem, equal, <u>direct</u>, <u>compare</u>; to compare, <u>be comparable</u>*. The word for "continually" is Strong's H8548 (tamiyd) - *continual, continuity*. The definition then for continuity is: *an uninterrupted succession or flow; a coherent whole*.

By integrating all of the aspects from these definitions of the Hebrew wording for this passage, we resolutely submit the following as a potential premise: To "order" the Menorah and the Table of Shewbread "continually" meant to arrange in an array prescribed by Yahweh – preparing them in some way in order to direct and ordain something. The priests were officially sanctioned by Yahweh to administer a continual ordering on a daily and weekly basis in the holy place of the Tabernacle. By comparing and contrasting Yahweh's prescribed ordering of the Menorah with that of the Table of Shewbread, the priests were shown how to maintain an uninterrupted succession or flow. From this flow, would then emerge the picture of a coherent whole, which we assert was Yahweh's calendar.

Breaking this Hebrew word down a bit more by getting a glimpse of its etymology, we gain even a bit more insight. The letters which compose "`arak" (the Hebrew word for "order") are "ayin", "resh", and "kaph". "Ayin" indicates: *well-spring, fountain, source and center relative to spiritual insight; watch, and know.* "Resh" suggests: *first, top, beginning, highest, head, chieftain, supreme one.* "Kaph" concludes this word with the implication of: *crowning accomplishment, and encompasses the whole of a thing, from the beginning to the end.*

It amplifies the concept that this ordering provides the well-spring fountain and source of a spiritual insight that the priests, as the head of the people, are to watch and know, encompassing the entirety of the matter. They were to understand Father's instructions for His calendar through this "ordering". This insight goes from the beginning of something clear through to the crowning accomplishment at the end. The spiritual insight that they are to watch and know emerges from the fountain as they order the menorah and the table of shewbread to form the calendar framework itself.

Perhaps the lights of the Menorah would log the 7 days of the week, and the Shewbread (being marked somehow with frankincense) would track the 12 months of the year. There would never be more or less than 7 days in the week, then it would resume the next count of 7. There would never be more or less than 12 months in the year, then it would resume the next count of 12. The Table of Shewbread had 2 rows of 6 loaves or cakes each. These 2 rows of 6 might well have represented the 2 sides of the year, 6 months in each. These 6-month periods would portray the flow of time from spring equinox (which ushers in the spring feasts in month 1) to the autumnal equinox (which brings forth the fall feasts in month 7), then the return from fall back to spring. From this emerging calendar picture, the priests were then fully equipped and authorized to delineate the ordained timing for Yahweh's feasts of Leviticus 23. Recall that feast days are numbered from the 1st day of the month. Passover is the 14th day of month 1, etc. It is simply a matter of counting to get from the beginning of the month to the specified day of a feast.

When was the Menorah and Table of Shewbread first put into use? We find the answer in Exodus:

Exodus 40:2-4
(2) **On the first day of the first month** <u>shalt thou set up the tabernacle</u> of the tent of the congregation.
(3) And thou shalt put therein the ark of the testimony, and cover the ark with the vail.
(4) And thou shalt **bring in the table, and set in order the things that are to be set in order upon it; and thou shalt bring in the candlestick, and light the lamps thereof**.

Indeed, this may have been the perpetual calendar designated by Yahweh on the 1st day of His calendar year to keep time from that day forward!

One of the key ways to recognize exceptional significance within a passage, is to notice that something within the passage is not a part of the expected flow of information. Such is the case in this Leviticus 24 passage. It seems to be very significant that the instructions regarding the continual ordering of the Menorah and the Table of Shewbread in Leviticus 24:1-9 is conspicuously tucked between the listing of the holy days in Leviticus 23 and the instructions for the Shemitah and Jubilee years in Leviticus 25. This passage about the Menorah and the Table of Shewbread was the only mention of Tabernacle implements found in this part of the Word at all. How could that be merely coincidental? Yahweh's Sabbath days in Leviticus 23 and His Sabbath years in Leviticus 25 are the very things that His perpetual calendar of Leviticus 24 would delineate.

Actually, there is an interesting interlude that follows the instructions for these Tabernacle implements. It is about a young man who was of partially Egyptian heritage. In this brief narrative, the young man is said to blaspheme the name of God and curse.

Leviticus 24:10-11
(10) And the son of an Israelitish woman, whose father was an Egyptian, went out among the children of Israel: and this son of the Israelitish woman and a man of Israel strove together in the camp;
(11) And the Israelitish woman's son **blasphemed** the **name** of the LORD, and **cursed**. And they brought him unto Moses: (and his mother's name was Shelomith, the daughter of Dibri, of the tribe of Dan:)

Three of the main words in verse 11 are all of interest as it relates to our subject matter. They are: blasphemed, name, and curse. The word "blasphemed" is Strong's H5344 (naqab) – *blasphemed, pierce through or strike through, bore – holes*. The word "name" is Strong's H8034 **(shem)** *name, report, reputation, fame, glory, monument, memorial*. It is thought to be from Strong's H7760 (suwm) - *put, lay, set, make, appoint, show, mark, regard, direct, ordain, establish, extend, constitute, determine, fix, station, put, set in place, plant, fix, transform into, constitute, fashion, work, bring to pass, appoint, to set or make for a sign*. The word "cursed" is Strong's H7043 (qalal) – *cursed, light thing, vile, despise, abated, make trifle or of little account, be lightly esteemed, make despicable*.

This young man was striving with a man of Israel. Though the text doesn't specifically mention what the strife was about, it appears that during the course of the conflict, the young man "blasphemed" the "name" of Yahweh and "cursed". While this may be literally true, there may be a secondary innuendo here. It follows DIRECTLY after the instructions for the Tabernacle implements, and there seems to be no reason for this positioning at all. Could its placement be significant? We could submit a possible scenario that would fit very well! The strife might have been relative to the use of the Tabernacle implements for calendar purposes. This narrative seems to be very out of character and out of place in this Chapter 24 text. Likewise, the entire Chapter 24 text seems to be out of place in reference to the surrounding text of Chapters 23 and 25 UNLESS you see it all in the framework of calendar keeping.

The young man who was accused had Egyptian heritage, and he had probably been schooled in the Egyptian ways. Could he have been disputing the priestly ways due to his understanding of Egyptian calendar keeping? The Britannica Encyclopedia - https://www.britannica.com/science/Egyptian-calendar -

In addition to this civil calendar, the ancient Egyptians simultaneously maintained a second calendar based upon the phases of the moon. The Egyptian lunar, the older of the two systems, consisted of twelve months whose duration differed according to the length of a full lunar cycle (normally 28 or 29 days). Each lunar month began with the new moon—reckoned from the first morning after the waning crescent had become invisible—and was named after the major festival celebrated within it. Since the lunar calendar was 10 or 11 days shorter than the solar year, a 13th month (called Thoth) was intercalated every several years to keep the lunar calendar in rough correspondence with the agricultural seasons and their feasts. New Year's Day was signaled by the annual heliacal rising of the star Sothis (Sirus), when it could be observed on the eastern horizon just before dawn in midsummer; the timing of this observation would determine whether or not the intercalary month would be employed.

This act of "blaspheming" Father's "name" and "cursing" then might actually have meant that he was piercing through, striking through and boring holes into the established report of Yahweh – what He had brought to pass, set up for a sign and ordained as the proper method of calendar keeping. This young man might have made light of Yahweh's way, esteemed it lightly, and even rendered it despicable. The penalty for doing so is said to be very harsh indeed. He was to be stoned. Perhaps Yahweh considers it blasphemous when the system He has established is blatantly disregarded.

Seeing it Come Together

The 7's and 12's then form a very cohesive, systematic and integrated structure to allow for perfect timekeeping by the priests. The Biblical text never mentions any specific observation of the moon, nor is there any prescribed method noted within or without the tabernacle for such observation. There is no actual reference to a full moon, a crescent moon, or any other phases of the moon whatsoever, except for the few seemingly misapplied English translations already mentioned of "chodesh(im)" as "new moon(s)". Actually, this carefully placed segment in the heart of the text about Father's holy days and His holy years indicates a calendar system based solely on arrangement and counting from the beginning of one year to its conclusion and the beginning of the next.

The position of the Menorah and the Table of Shewbread so near the Holy of Holies shows the importance of this timing system to Yahweh. It would be the method by which His holy patterning was to be maintained so His holy days would be honored at the proper times. It would be His sacred calendar system. Any disruption in the sacred flow of 7's and 12's in Yahweh's time-keeping structure would cause distortion of His calendar.

The tabernacle, along with the implements of it were to be designed in accordance with Yahweh's specific patterning. The provision of this patterning to Moses was recorded in Exodus, and it was confirmed yet again in Hebrews:

Exodus 25:8-9
(8) And let them make me a sanctuary; that I may dwell among them.
(9) According to all that **I shew thee**, after the pattern of the tabernacle, and the **pattern of all the instruments thereof**, even so shall ye make it.

Hebrews 8:5
(5) Who serve unto the example and shadow of heavenly things, as Moses was admonished of God when he was about to make the tabernacle: for, See, saith he, that thou make all things **according to the pattern shewed to thee** in the mount.

Perhaps even the intricate patterning of 7s in the bowls, knops, and flowers within the Menorah itself would aid the priests in tracking the 7 sets of 7 in the count to Pentecost and to Jubilee. Indeed, it looks as though the Menorah and Table of Shewbread were made by Yahweh's specified pattern to serve as the priest's perpetual calendar. If this be the case, perhaps we should be gleaning from Yahweh's ordained pattern so we can maintain the calendar Yahweh provided for the human race until His patterns are concluded at the end of time itself!

Yahweh's patterning of 7's has a purpose. Not only is it concretely established, but it is profoundly displayed repeatedly in His space-time fabric, and it is evident throughout the Bible as His number for timing sequence. It is actually the pattern that concludes His designation for time itself at the completion of the 7th millennial day in our world. The number 8 is strongly associated with "transcendence" in Hebraic reckoning. Indeed, it will be the 8th millennial day when we transcend into the realm without time. It is only at this instant of transcendence when the cycles we know in our world will cease their perpetual spiraling momentum, and 8 will begin a new segment of time rather than reverting back to one to continue the earthly spiral. Yet while we are here, the 8th day after the completion of the 7-day week that foreshadows these millennial days is also the 1st day of the following week. As long as we remain in this 3-D realm, the patterns of 7 must follow one another without alteration.

Finally, when the 7th millennial day is completed, we will exit this 3-D realm and enter one where there is no longer any time as we know it, so another millennial day that is governed by the physics of space/time will not be started. Only then will Yahweh's sacred 7 patterning be concluded as we step into the timelessness of eternity future.

CHAPTER 13

SEVENS, TWELVES, AND INTERCALARY ADJUSTMENTS

We had become aware that sevens and twelves both seemed to be critical to Father's calendar patterning. What about thirty-day months? Wouldn't something need to give somewhere when we had to periodically adjust to the actual duration of the solar year?

How Long are Biblical Months?

In numerous places, the Bible also mentions strings of days that are easily divided into 30-day months. For this reason, 30-day months too are significant. An example might be "a thousand two hundred and threescore days" (1260 days) in Revelation 12:6. This is thought to be a period of 3-1/2 years (implied by Revelation 12:14), matching the 42 ("forty and two") months in Revelation 11:2. The reference of 42 months matches the reference of 1260 days only if each month is 30 days long. Other Scriptural references also seem to imply association between 30 days and the length of a month. It is a commonly quoted period of time. So, the theory goes that Yahweh's months are to be 30 days each, and some extend this out to say that there should be ONLY 12 30-day months in the year each year.

A problem occurs here though. In a single year where there are 12 months of 30 days each without any adjustment, the year would be 360 days. This is 5.242 days shorter than the actual solar year. In a period of just 3-1/2 years, as illustrated above, the solar year would be out of sync by some 18.347 days. It doesn't take much effort to see where this would lead over longer periods of time. The harvests would very soon be in the wrong time of year to align to Yahweh's agriculturally based festival seasons! The barley would not be available to wave when it would be needed. It is immediately obvious then that this could never be His intent.

At the risk of sounding repetitious, we will emphasize once again in summary form that the harvest is dependent upon the sun – not the calendar. Yahweh's harvest periods are indelibly linked to the position of the sun in the solar year. Likewise, the barley which must be waved as the first fruits offering is unalterably linked to the arrival of spring and its associated harvest period. The month of Abib must correlate to this harvest, so it must begin at the right time of year for the sun to carry out its harvest function. Father's calendar year must begin at the appropriate time in the solar year so the harvest season and their associated festival dates can proceed on schedule. As long as our solar years remain 365.242 days in length, intercalary days must be applied periodically so Father's calendar year will begin at the right time to align to the actual solar year.

Realizing the necessity of adjusting to the solar year, we must determine where these adjustments are to occur. There are 3 timing elements determined by the celestial signs of Genesis 1:14: days, seasons, and years. Conversely, there are two perpetual (thus static and inflexible) timing elements that have no bearing on celestial signs, but they must simply be counted. They are the weeks and months indicated by the Menorah and the Table of Shewbread in Leviticus 24. Together, these provide the 5 elements of time: days, weeks, months, seasons, and years; and some cyclical relationships exist between them. There are 24 hours in the day, 7 days in the week, 30 days in the month, 12 months in the year, and 4 seasons in the year. All of these cycles must co-exist together to form our calendars.

There are only and always 7 lights on Yahweh's ordained Menorah, just as there are never more or less than 7 days in the week. Likewise, there are never 11 or 13 loaves of Shewbread but only and always there are 12 loaves. The 12-month year then would be a constant as well. As a side note to somewhat validate this concept, there is never a mention of a 13th month in the Bible. By piecing together Esther 9:1 & 17 we see that the celebration of Purim is to be in the twelfth month of the year. Yet, when the extra month (a 13th month) of the Jewish calendar is inserted in our era, Purim is celebrated that month. That would appear to be a significant discrepancy in the Scriptural observance of Purim. If a 13th month was periodically to be added, this Biblical text would surely address when to celebrate on such years.

The book of Esther also seems to indicate simply a 12-month cycle in chapter 2:

Esther 2:12
(12) Now when every maid's turn was come to go in to king Ahasuerus, after that she had been twelve months, according to the manner of the women, (for so were the days of their purifications accomplished, to wit, six months with oil of myrrh, and six months with sweet odours, and with other things for the purifying of the women;)

This 12-month period would comprise a full year of preparation, and it also implies the 2 6-month segments relative to the equinox cycles as well, just as we see in the Table of Shewbread. It is likely the year of purification began with the vernal equinox to the autumnal equinox, designated for "oil of myrrh". It would then conclude from the autumnal equinox back to the vernal equinox, during which "sweet odours" and "other things for the purifying of the women" were applied. The culmination of this 12-month period then would make her appropriately pure for presentation to the King for marriage at the vernal equinox of the following year. The commentary on the book of Esther in Gill's Exposition of the Entire Bible relates that kings were not to marry at any other time than the vernal equinox.

The Book of Jubilees validates Yahweh's sacred flow of 7's a bit more by showing us that His year is to have only complete weeks. No remaining days of the week are to be left at the end of the year to interrupt the sacred flow of 7's within the year, so the days in the year must be divisible by 7. How then do we correlate that to 12 30-day months? It could never work, as 30 is not equally divisible by 7. The math shows us that it cannot work. Or can it?

We can continue to have 30 days in each month, but we will simply have to adjust the cycle intermittently. This is accomplished by applying an intercalary day which does not disrupt the sacred flows, yet it induces harmony with the solar year. How do we do this? Before addressing the solution, there is one more consideration. The Book of Jubilees seems to show us that Yahweh's seasons are also sacred. He ordained the Heavenly display to decree them. Each seasonal quarter of the year is to have only completed weeks within it as well. This means that the number of days in the quarter must also be divisible by 7. Since the 12 months in the year is another static sacred flow, it cannot fluctuate. There are 4 quarters in the year, making 3 months in a quarter. There are 90 days in three 30-day months. This would be 12 weeks and 6 days. We would only need 91 days in the quarter to make 13 complete weeks. A single extra day per quarter is needed.

As we see it, the foundational structuring of time in Yahweh's calendar would be based on the perpetual continuance of the 7-day week and the 12-month year. Therefore, intercalary days must be placed in such a way that this sacred perpetual nature is never disrupted. We have illustrated repeatedly how the 7's are designated spokes of time which Yahweh established as an unremitting pattern. Likewise, we see the 12's as being a sacred time interval for months as well. The 7th day is to cycle back around to the 1st, and the 12th month is to cycle back around to the 1st without exception. These two specifically established spokes of time are continually repetitive in their patterning. The ceaseless continuation of these two spokes of time cannot be disrupted without distorting the entire fabric of Fathers calendar framework.

There simply is no mechanism in place to validate the same type of sacred flow between the 30-day month cycles that we find for the 7's and 12's in Leviticus. It is this 30-day succession which must be amended intermittently to keep the others static and to complete the calendar picture.

It seems that a single rule to structure this cohesion for this calendar would be that **no intercalary day or days can ever disrupt the sacred flow of 7's or 12's.** Instead, they will act as an adhesive to glue together the 30-day months in 4 equalized segments. The Book of Jubilees shows us how such adjustments are to be made to align Yahweh's calendar to our solar years. A single day is added at the end of each 3 months to make 91-day quarters with equal weeks. In this way, they complete the year without disrupting the sacred flows of Yahweh's spokes of time, His 7's and His 12's. Such intervening intercalary days at these junctures actually create a cohesive whole in a way that could not otherwise be accomplished. We see then that there are 12 months of 30 days each in the Zadokite calendar along with 4 strategically placed intercalary days in the standard year.

Our Gregorian calendars don't make a separate page for the intercalary day being added each 4th year. For convenience sake, they just tack it onto the end of February. In a similar manner, the Zadokite calendar shows an extra day tacked onto each 3rd month. It does not mean that those months are viewed as 31-day months. They are still considered to be 30-day months, just as February is still considered to be a 28-day month.

Such intercalary days are sometimes referenced as being "out of time" with other calendar systems. This seems to be appropriate here as well, because they complete the year without disrupting the sacred flows of 7's and 12's, Yahweh's spokes of time. In this manner, they maintain the integrity of Father's 7's and 12's patterning, while providing a perfect Sabbath calendar each year.

The tracking of 7's and 12's is carefully preserved in The Book of Jubilees. This book also provides a detailed log of Father's weekly Sabbaths, His holy days and His years of Jubilee for our historical reference. The implication seems strong that the 7 branch Menorah and the 2 rows of 6 loaves each (12 loaves) could have been Father's ordained method for the priests to track these specific time frames.

The Sabbath-based year must be completed with the inclusion of 4 intercalary days. By placing one at the end of each quarter, the entire calendar fits together as a continual uninterrupted succession or flow of continuity that forms a coherent whole. (Where have we heard that before?) This whole is a calendar year that meets all of the criteria and also adjusts to the solar year. On occasion, an extra "week of days" or full week will also be needed at the end of the year. Again, these 7 intercalary days do not disrupt the flows of 7's and 12's, and they adhere Yahweh's religious calendar to the reality of His actual solar year. The timing of this adjustment is to be determined by the arrival of the spring equinox marker. Even then there will be no interruption of continuity within the 7-day weeks and 12 months of 30 days each, as the extra days will be "out of time. The Zadokite calendar will provide a coherent and complete calendar package.

The Biblical Calendar Then and Now

Those who advocate 12 months of 30 days must eventually concede to have these intercalary days inserted somewhere. No matter where they are placed, the flow of 30's must at some point in the year be altered. Whether it is one time (all intercalary days being inserted at the end of the year) or 4 times (1 day being placed at the end of each quarter), the flow of 30's must of necessity be interrupted. Otherwise Yahweh's religious year quickly loses its correlation to the reality of His solar year. There is simply no way around it. The 30-day month cycle must <u>always</u> yield to the reality of the solar year by applying the extra days at some point in time, so the succession of 30-day cycles must be altered to maintain alignment. Though the 30-day month is certainly a Biblical standard, there is simply no established pattern for perpetually progressive 30-day counts as we are shown for 7-day weeks and 12-month years in Yahweh's patterning. To place them all at the end of the year would leave the seasonal quarters with uneven weeks. It would also place the feast days of the latter half of the year on the wrong days according to <u>The Book of Jubilees</u> designation.

<u>The Book of Jubilees</u> specifies that these adjustments occur at Yahweh's sacred seasonal junctures – one per quarter. This separates the quarters into special segments and allow for a day to celebrate His sacred seasons. Each is special in His sight.

Because each quarter ends in even weeks, the schema of the calendar formation for each season (quarter) of the year is identical. The duration of the seasons easily overlay one another, repeating themselves in a cyclical motion. This is yet another example of the simplicity of Yahweh's intended cyclical patterning.

The ending of every season and year in exact weeks also means that each of Yahweh's feast days will fall on a specific weekday each and every year. For instance, Feast of Tabernacles will always begin on Wednesday - no exceptions. The timing of this calendar assures that none of Yahweh's 3-day "chodesh" events or His annual holy days will ever fall on the weekly Sabbath, so no weekly Sabbath period is interrupted with the celebrations of any change of seasons ("chodeshim") or any of Yahweh's feast days ("chodeshim"). His seasonal transitions, His annual holy days, and His weekly Sabbaths, all have their individual places. They flow with perfect synchronous conformity on His calendar.

The 364-day calendar year always goes by the 7 days of Yahweh's creation week with a primary focus on weekday 4 (Wednesday) to honor the 4th day of creation when Yahweh set His clock in the heavens. Therefore, the new calendar year always begins on a weekday 4 (Wednesday). When the new vernal equinox arrives, we advance to the very next weekday 4 (Wednesday) and start the new year. The 364 days will always end on a weekday 3 (Tuesday). If the equinox has not occurred by sundown the following day (which is weekday 4), then an extra week is added. If the vernal equinox should occur on that weekday 4 (Wednesday), then sundown is the determining factor. If it occurs prior to sundown, no extra week is needed. If it occurs after sundown, then it is reckoned that the equinox was actually on weekday 5, and we advance to the following weekday 4 (Wednesday) to begin the new year (adding the extra week).

The weeks always start on a weekday 1, and the year always starts on a weekday 4. Subsequently, each seasonal quarter also starts on a weekday 4. This assures that Yahweh's creation week is always complete and the change of year never disrupts His Sabbath schedule since the year always has 52 or 53 complete weeks. This then keeps Yahweh's patterning intact in every respect, properly honoring His Sabbaths and keeping His seasons on course with the sun. Therefore, the crops will be ready at the right times.

Ezekiel speaks of a wheel with a wheel:

Ezekiel 1:15-16

(15) Now as I beheld the living creatures, behold <u>one wheel upon the earth</u> by the living creatures, <u>with his four faces</u>.

(16) The appearance of the wheels and their work was like unto the colour of a beryl: and they four <u>had one likeness</u>: and their appearance and their work was as it were <u>a wheel in the middle of a wheel</u>.

This cryptic passage may provide the meat for several different typologies, but one very loosely based typology might serve to show the relativity of time. Again, we see the principle of Yahweh's cyclical patterning being demonstrated. Imagine for a moment that the 4 creatures who had 1 likeness could be the 4 seasons within the wheel of the year. Likewise, are the other wheels within. We could see the wheels keeping **complete weeks** <u>within</u> **complete seasons** <u>within</u> **complete years** – all in the concise and neatly ordered, continuously flowing and structured package ordained by Father. When the patterning of sacred 7's is kept intact, these timing aspects fall into alignment. The 2 equinoxes and the 2 solstices provide the 4 quarter segments, and the sacred week is fully completed before moving from one season or quarter to the next, or from one year to the next. Likewise, the historical documentation within <u>The Book of Jubilees</u> serves to substantiate this ordering. Again, we will re-quote a segment from its pages to refresh its message in our hearts:

<u>The Book of Jubilees</u> 6:29 - <u>The Researchers Library of Ancient Texts Volume 1</u> - by R.H. Charles, Oxford – p. 288 -

*And <u>they placed them on the heavenly tablets,</u> **<u>each had thirteen weeks</u>**<u>; from one to another</u> (passed) their memorial, from the first to the second, and from the second to the third, and from the third to the fourth.*

Each of the 4 quarters of the year will have EXACTLY 13 full weeks, just as the year is to have EXACTLY 52 full weeks. Only when we have the 91 (13 X 7) day quarters is there 13 full weeks in the quarter. It is simply a matter of realizing the sacredness of Yahweh's patterning.

CHAPTER 14

DETERMINING FATHER'S HOLY DAYS

Coming to terms with the working of this OLD calendar system, we were amazed to find the simplicity of its structure. Putting it all together was elementary in nature. It took very little effort at all! Best of all, it was confirmed in historical data.

Dates on the Zadokite Calendar

Again, the flow and counting of this calendar system provides ultimate simplicity.

An outline of Yahweh's decreed Annual Sabbath feast dates is the same every year. It is always as follows:

I-14 is Passover - always on weekday 3 (Tuesday).
I-15 is 1st day of Unleavened Bread - always on weekday 4 (Wednesday).
I-21 is 7th day of Unleavened Bread - always on weekday 3 (Tuesday).
I-26 is waving of the first fruits barley sheaf - always on weekday 1 (Sunday).
    This is the day that begins the 50-day omer count to Pentecost.
    (We will cover a bit later why this is one week later than is typically taught.) III-15 is Pentecost - always on weekday 1 (Sunday).
VII-1 is Feast of Trumpets - always on weekday 4 (Wednesday).
VII-10 is Day of Atonement - always on weekday 6 (Friday).
VII-15 is 1st day of Feast of Tabernacles - always on weekday 4 (Wednesday).
VII-22 is 8th day of Feast of Tabernacles - always on weekday 4 (Wednesday).

Incidental feast dates not specified by Yahweh are:

IX-25 is 1st day of Chanukkah - always on weekday 4 (Wednesday).
X-1 is 8th day of Chanukkah - always on weekday 4 (Wednesday).
XII-14 is Purim - always on weekday 7 (Saturday).
XII-15 is Shushan Purim - always on weekday 1 (Sunday).

The four seasonal transitions are:

XII-30, XII-31, & I-1 – spring equinox observation
III-30, III-31, & IV-1 – summer solstice observation
VI-30, VI-31, & VII-1 – autumnal equinox observation
IX-30, IX-31, & X – 1 – winter solstice observation

All four transitions are always on the month days 30 and 31 of the ending month and day one of the following month. The weekdays they fall on are always weekdays 2, 3, & 4 (Monday, Tuesday, and Wednesday).

CHAPTER 15

COMPLICATIONS?

When we pulled it all together and confirmed it with the writings of old, we found a couple of disturbing aspects. Some of the specific timing did not concur with commonly viewed time frames. However, did they conflict Biblically? At one point, we were ready to throw it all out, but when we did our homework in the Bible, we found that there was not only a lack of conflict, but further verification of the timing on this calendar.

But What About the Timing for the Sheaf Offering on this Calendar?

For those who are schooled in Hebrew Roots, there are a couple of issues that seem to stand out here, regarding the timing of Passover and the waving of the sheaf. When we come to understand how all of this unfolds, it actually serves to solidify the case for this calendar!

We'll begin with the day of waving the barley sheaf, and the subsequent timing for the day of Pentecost (as they are listed on the outline). The waving of the barley sheaf is about a week later than is traditionally taught. It is traditionally taught that the day of the waving must occur within the week of Unleavened Bread. However, is that what Scripture says? Let's examine the surrounding text, noting the pause in context between verses 8 and 9:

Leviticus 23:5-16
(5) In the fourteenth day of the first month at even is the LORD'S passover.
(6) And on the 15th day of the same month is the feast of unleavened bread unto the LORD: seven days ye must eat unleavened bread.
(7) In the first day ye shall have an holy convocation: ye shall do no servile work therein.
(8) But ye shall offer an offering made by fire unto the LORD seven days: in the seventh day is an holy convocation: ye shall do no servile work therein.
(9) And the LORD spake unto Moses, saying,
(10) Speak unto the children of Israel, and say unto them, <u>When ye be come into the land which I give unto you, and shall **reap the harvest** thereof, **then ye shall bring a sheaf of the firstfruits** of your harvest unto the priest:</u>
(11) <u>And he shall wave the sheaf before the LORD, to be accepted for you: on the morrow after the sabbath the priest shall wave it.</u>
(12) And ye shall offer that day when ye wave the sheaf an he lamb without blemish of the first year for a burnt offering unto the LORD.
(13) And the meat offering thereof shall be two tenth deals of fine flour mingled with oil, an offering made by fire unto the LORD for a sweet savour: and the drink offering thereof shall be of wine, the fourth part of an hin.
(14) And ye shall eat neither bread, nor parched corn, nor green ears, until the selfsame day that ye have

brought an offering unto your God: it shall be a statute for ever throughout your generations in all your dwellings.

(15) And ye shall count unto you from the morrow after the sabbath, from the day that ye brought the sheaf of the wave offering; seven sabbaths shall be complete:

(16) Even unto the morrow after the seventh sabbath shall ye number fifty days; and ye shall offer a new meat offering unto the LORD.

Notice that verses 5-8 encompass Passover and Unleavened Bread, detailing the sacrificial criteria for that week. Then verse 9 detaches the latter part of the passage from the former by beginning afresh with a totally separate exposition: "And the LORD spake unto Moses, saying, …". Father then relates the means of dealing with the wave sheaf, which involves a totally different offering than what is mandated for Passover and Unleavened Bread. There is no indication here that this day of waving of the first fruits intersects with the holy week of Unleavened Bread at all, and the contextual inference is actually that it does not. It is related Scripturally only to the reaping of the harvest, at which time the first fruits sheaf of that harvest is presented to the priest so that he can offer it to Father. Indeed, this does seem to fit the pattern of the calendar used by the Essenes.

Though the I-26 date for the waving of the sheaf by the Essenes is certain, the reason for it being done after the week of Unleavened Bread is not. When trying to piece it together, we could find only reasonable speculation. Apparently. the week of Unleavened Bread was observed as a festive occasion throughout, and no harvesting was done until the week was completed. The final day of the set aside week of Unleavened Bread was on I-21, which was always on a weekday 3 (Tuesday). This gave them from weekday 4 (Wednesday) until sundown on weekday 6 (Friday) that week to gather in the first of their harvest and compose a sheaf of the very best of the crop. They then rested on weekday 7 (Saturday, the weekly Sabbath), and presented their sheaf for waving on I-26 - weekday 1 (Sunday). This then would be the day that would begin the 50-day counting of the omer, and it would conclude at Pentecost on III-15 – also a weekday 1 (Sunday).

In applying New Testament meaning to this wave sheaf offering, the current Hebrew Roots understanding sees Y'shua as the fulfillment of the Passover Lamb and then the first fruits of the dead:

1 Corinthians 5:7

(7) Purge out therefore the old leaven, that ye may be a new lump, as ye are unleavened. For even Christ our passover is sacrificed for us:

1 Corinthians 15:20

(20) But now is Christ risen from the dead, and become the firstfruits of them that slept.

A typological application in which Y'shua is the first fruits of the dead is generally understood from these verses. The first fruits sheaf of the barley harvest then represents the first fruits harvest of those who have "slept" (were dead), and have been resurrected. All of this is absolutely the case! Accordingly, they see the necessity for the waving of the barley first fruits sheaf immediately after Y'shua's resurrection. The empty tomb was found on Sunday during the week of Unleavened Bread. It is then presumed that He ascended to Heaven and was waved before Father that same day. Correlating this to the waving of the barley sheaf, it is then taught that the sheaf must be waved on the Sunday during the week of Unleavened bread. However, there may be more to consider here.

Since the earthly is patterned after the Heavenly, this may not be true. If Y'shua was presented before Father at that time, it might have been to begin the transition from the Pascal Lamb to our High Priest. Maybe the waving did not occur until that transition was completed and His priestly role was implemented. There might actually be a legally required 7-day period to consecrate Y'shua for service as our High Priest. This earthly pattern is found in Exodus:

Exodus 29:29-35
(29) And the holy garments of Aaron shall be his sons' after him, to be anointed therein, and to be consecrated in them.
(30) And that son that is priest in his stead shall put them on <u>seven days</u>, when he cometh into the tabernacle of the congregation to minister in the holy place.
(31) And thou shalt take the ram of the consecration, and seethe his flesh in the holy place.
(32) And Aaron and his sons shall eat the flesh of the ram, and the bread that is in the basket, by the door of the tabernacle of the congregation.
(33) And they shall eat those things wherewith the atonement was made, to consecrate and to sanctify them: but a stranger shall not eat thereof, because they are holy.
(34) And if ought of the flesh of the consecrations, or of the bread, remain unto the morning, then thou shalt burn the remainder with fire: it shall not be eaten, because it is holy.
(35) And thus shalt thou do unto Aaron, and to his sons, according to all things which I have commanded thee: <u>seven days shalt thou consecrate them</u>.

Since the earthly was patterned after the heavenly, would this not mean that the heavenly version would be of the same nature? The 7 days of unleavened bread (which represents sinlessness) might actually be representative of this consecration period for the One who was to transition from our sacrificial lamb to our High Priest.

Furthermore, Y'shua had been in contact with defiled man, taken on that sin, and had been subjected to eath itself. Even His contact with the grave is significant. Those in contact with the dead or the grave were also to undergo a 7-day period before they were considered to be ceremonially clean:

Numbers 19:11
(11) He that toucheth the dead body of any man shall be <u>unclean seven days</u>.

Numbers 19:18-19
(18) And a clean person shall take hyssop, and dip it in the water, and sprinkle it upon the tent, and upon all the vessels, and upon the persons that were there, and <u>upon him that touched a bone, or one slain, or one dead, or a grave</u>:
(19) And the clean person shall sprinkle upon the unclean on the third day, and on the seventh day: <u>and on the seventh day he shall purify himself, and wash his clothes, and bathe himself in water, and shall be clean at even</u>.

Please note that this was a matter of becoming CEREMONIALLY clean. The man who touched a grave would not be spiritually unclean for having done so, as it would not have been a sin by that man. There is simply a ceremonial aspect of a 7-day purification period that is needed to be cleansed and consecrated from Father's holy perspective that we do not fully understand. It seems that this would be especially significant when His pattern is applied in the Heavenly Kingdom to prepare Y'shua for the duties of High Priest. Though Y'shua was totally sinless in His walk and was never <u>spiritually</u> defiled in ANY respect whatsoever, He would still likely have to be <u>ceremonially</u> purified for His office as our High Priest.

Then we see something else that makes a bit of sense relative to this time frame. Hebrews tells us that AS our High Priest, Y'shua must also have a first fruits offering to offer (wave). Referring to Y'shua, Hebrews tells us:

Hebrews 8:3
(3) For every high priest is ordained to offer gifts and sacrifices: wherefore it is of necessity that this man have somewhat also to offer.

What might He offer to Father as His first fruits to be waved? Recall that the Bible often associates people instead of grain as a type of harvest. Maybe it is a first fruits sheaf of people that the new High Priest of the people was to wave before Father as His harvest offering. As we have seen with Y'shua, the timing of the barley harvest is linked to the resurrection from the dead. We would also remember the verse that tells of the graves being opened at Y'shua's resurrection and those within being seen alive:

Matthew 27:52-53
(52) And the graves were opened; and many bodies of the saints which slept arose,
(53) And came out of the graves after his resurrection, and went into the holy city, and appeared unto many.

The Bible isn't clear regarding the duration of the visitation in the holy city of these resurrected saints, or what happened to them after that. It just specifies that they came out of their graves after Y'shua's resurrection, and they appeared to many. On the 8th day (the 1st day of the FOLLOWING week), Y'shua would be totally cleansed AND consecrated simultaneously. After the fulfillment of this 7-day period from his death experience, Y'shua would be ceremonially cleansed and ready to be waved before Father. He would also be ready after 7 days of ceremonial consecration to serve as our new High Priest and wave the first fruits of His harvest of resurrected saints.

The waving of the sheaf on weekday 1 (Sunday) I-26 (a full week after his resurrection) would allow for the fulfillment of His ceremonial cleansing and consecration. The waving before the throne at the end of this week would then be perfectly in sync with the waving of the barley first fruits here on earth on I-26 on the Zadokite calendar rather than on the Sunday during Unleavened Bread.

Y'shua was then able to return to earth and take up where he left off. Thomas (one of his disciples) had not been with the other disciples when Y'shua first appeared to the disciples. When the others told Thomas what had happened, Thomas didn't believe them. He said he wouldn't be convinced until he could touch Y'shua's wounds:

John 20:24-25
(24) But Thomas, one of the twelve, called Didymus, was not with them when Jesus came.
(25) The other disciples therefore said unto him, We have seen the Lord. But he said unto them, Except I shall see in his hands the print of the nails, and put my finger into the print of the nails, and thrust my hand into his side, I will not believe.

It is notable that there was a delay of a week between his first appearance to the disciples and his next appearance to them. It would have been AFTER the conclusion of His week of consecration and the waving that followed on day 8 that He would return to satisfy Thomas:

John 20:26

(26) And <u>after eight days</u> again his disciples were within, and Thomas with them: then came Jesus, the doors being shut, and stood in the midst, and said, Peace be unto you.

Y'shua would have known of the doubting of Thomas. If He had not been otherwise occupied in Heaven, He would likely have addressed this sooner with Thomas rather than leaving him in his state of doubt and confusion.

Leviticus & Joshua Provide the Picture

A dear brother in Y'shua, Randy, has provided the breadcrumbs for us to verify that the first fruits barley sheaf of Joshua's day could not possibly have been waved during the week of Unleavened Bread. This is substantial confirmation of the information in the Dead Sea Scrolls that indicates the wave sheaf is to be presented the following week. The breadcrumbs Randy provide begin in the book of Joshua, so that's where we'll start. The evidence is presented below; we just need to follow the timing of events to see how this is so. Before getting into particulars though, we will present the entire pertinent passage of Joshua so the timing of events can be easily followed. (Note that the underlining actually serves to provide a shortcut - an abbreviated narrative overview to save some time if you prefer.)

Joshua 5:11-6:20

(11) And <u>they did eat of the old corn</u> of the land <u>on the morrow after the passover</u>, unleavened cakes, and parched corn in the selfsame day.

(12) And the manna ceased on the morrow after they had eaten of the old corn of the land; neither had the children of Israel manna any more; but they did eat of the fruit of the land of Canaan that year.

(13) <u>And it came to pass, when Joshua was by Jericho</u>, that he lifted up his eyes and looked, and, behold, there stood a man over against him with his sword drawn in his hand: and Joshua went unto him, and said unto him, Art thou for us, or for our adversaries?

(14) And he said, Nay; but as captain of the host of the LORD am I now come. And Joshua fell on his face to the earth, and did worship, and said unto him, What saith my lord unto his servant?

(15) And the captain of the LORD'S host said unto Joshua, Loose thy shoe from off thy foot; for the place whereon thou standest is holy. And Joshua did so.

(1) Now Jericho was straitly shut up because of the children of Israel: none went out, and none came in.

(2) And <u>the LORD said unto Joshua, See, I have given into thine hand Jericho</u>, and the king thereof, and the mighty men of valour.

(3) And <u>ye shall compass the city</u>, all ye men of war, and go round about the city once. Thus shalt thou do <u>six days</u>.

(4) And seven priests shall bear before the ark seven trumpets of rams' horns: <u>and the seventh day</u> ye shall <u>compass the city seven times</u>, and the priests shall blow with the trumpets.

(5) And it shall come to pass, that when they make a long blast with the ram's horn, and when ye hear the sound of the trumpet, all the people shall shout with a great shout; <u>and the wall of the city shall fall down flat</u>, and the people shall ascend up every man straight before him.

(6) <u>And Joshua the son of Nun called the priests</u>, and said unto them, Take up the ark of the covenant, and let seven priests bear seven trumpets of rams' horns before the ark of the LORD.

(7) <u>And he said unto the people</u>, Pass on, and <u>compass the city, and let him that is armed pass on before the ark of the LORD</u>.

(8) And it came to pass, when Joshua had spoken unto the people, that the seven priests bearing the seven trumpets of rams' horns passed on before the LORD, and blew with the trumpets: and the ark of the covenant of the LORD followed them.

(9) And the armed men went before the priests that blew with the trumpets, and the rereward came after the ark, the priests going on, and blowing with the trumpets.

(10) And Joshua had commanded the people, saying, Ye shall not shout, nor make any noise with your voice, neither shall any word proceed out of your mouth, until the day I bid you shout; then shall ye shout.

(11) So the ark of the LORD compassed the city, going about it once: and they came into the camp, and lodged in the camp.

(12) And Joshua rose early in the morning, and the priests took up the ark of the LORD.

(13) And seven priests bearing seven trumpets of rams' horns before the ark of the LORD went on continually, and blew with the trumpets: and the armed men went before them; but the rereward came after the ark of the LORD, the priests going on, and blowing with the trumpets.

(14) And the second day they compassed the city once, and returned into the camp: so they did six days.

(15) And it came to pass on the seventh day, that they rose early about the dawning of the day, and compassed the city after the same manner seven times: only on that day they compassed the city seven times.

(16) And it came to pass at the seventh time, when the priests blew with the trumpets, Joshua said unto the people, Shout; for the LORD hath given you the city.

(17) And the city shall be accursed, even it, and all that are therein, to the LORD: only Rahab the harlot shall live, she and all that are with her in the house, because she hid the messengers that we sent.

(18) And ye, in any wise keep yourselves from the accursed thing, lest ye make yourselves accursed, when ye take of the accursed thing, and make the camp of Israel a curse, and trouble it.

(19) But all the silver, and gold, and vessels of brass and iron, are consecrated unto the LORD: they shall come into the treasury of the LORD.

(20) So the people shouted when the priests blew with the trumpets: and it came to pass, when the people heard the sound of the trumpet, and the people shouted with a great shout, that the wall fell down flat, so that the people went up into the city, every man straight before him, and they took the city.

So, let's piece a few things together by connecting the dots:

- The day after Passover, Joshua and the people ate of the OLD corn of the land where they were (Joshua 5:11). We should note that the word for "old corn" in this verse is a single Hebrew word: Strong's H5669 (`abuwr) - *passed, i.e. kept over; **used only of stored grain**: - old corn.* It is notable that some translations do not designate "old" here, which is strange, since the actual meaning of the term "abuwr" means only grain which has been stored and kept over – old.

- The use of the term "green ears" in Leviticus 23:14 reveals that God's people were to refrain from eating anything from the new harvest produce until after the sheaf was waved.

Leviticus 23:14

(14) And ye shall eat neither bread, nor parched corn, nor **green ears**, until the selfsame day that ye have brought an offering unto your God: it shall be a statute for ever throughout your generations in all your dwellings.

- So - if the first fruits barley sheaf had not yet been waved, (and we'll see why this was so) we can understand why they were still eating of the "old corn" in Joshua 5:11.

- Leviticus also specifies that the first fruits barley sheaf waving is to occur AFTER they come into the land **which Father gives them** and they reap the harvest there.

Leviticus 23:10

(10) Speak unto the children of Israel, and say unto them, <u>When ye be come into the land</u> **which I give unto you**, <u>and shall reap the harvest thereof</u>, **then** ye shall bring a sheaf of the firstfruits of your harvest unto the priest:

- We will see that they had not yet entered the land which Father would give them, so they could not have reaped the harvest or waved the first fruits barley sheaf.

- Joshua 6:2 knits with Leviticus 23:10 to show that Jericho was to be the land the Father had promised to give them – the land where they were to reap the harvest, and THEN they could wave the first fruits barley sheaf. The remainder of the passage details what their approach to victory was to be.

- The order is clearly progressive. Before they could reap the harvest and wave the sheaf, they must first be given the land by Father!

- Joshua 5:11 shows us that they ate of the old corn on the morrow after Passover.

- <u>Passover is day 14 of the 1st month, so the day they ate of the old corn must have been day 15 of the 1st month.</u>

- Progression of events then mandates that the instructions could not have been given, and the marching could not have begun <u>PRIOR to day 15 of the 1st month</u>.

- Was there a lapse of time between the eating of the old corn in Joshua 5:11 and the timing when Joshua stood by Jericho and received his instructions in 5:13-6:5? There is certainly room to speculate that the receiving of instructions might not have been immediately after the eating of the old corn, but <u>because the narrative flows rather seamlessly, we know that there would not have been much of a lapse</u>. Due to the absence of a direct Scriptural answer to this question, we simply cannot peg this march to specific calendar days with certainty, but there is much we can conclude:

- We know that <u>Unleavened Bread covers a seven-day period (days 15-21 of the 1st month)</u>.

Leviticus 23:6

(6) And on the <u>fifteenth day of the same month</u> is the <u>feast of unleavened bread</u> unto the LORD: <u>seven days</u> ye must eat unleavened bread.

- Because the march could not have started until at least day 15 of the 1st month, and it took 7 days, then the earliest day the march could have ended would be <u>day 21 of the 1st month, the last day of Unleavened Bread</u>.

- Since they could not enter the land, reap the harvest, and provide a first fruits barley sheaf to wave until then, <u>the waving could not have happened until after day 21 of the 1st month, the last day of Unleavened Bread</u>.

- Therefore, <u>the waving of the first fruits barley sheaf could not have been during the Week of Unleavened Bread</u>. Only AFTER the march had ended and the land had been given to them, could they begin to reap and provide a sheaf to be waved.

- The first fruits barley sheaf must be waved on a morrow after a weekly Sabbath to start the countdown to Shavuot - in order that Shavuot (fifty days later) would also be the morrow after a Sabbath.

Leviticus 23:15-16
(15) And ye shall count unto you <u>from the morrow after the sabbath, from the day that ye brought the sheaf of the wave offering; seven sabbaths shall be complete</u>:
(16) Even <u>unto the morrow after the seventh sabbath</u> shall ye number fifty days; and ye shall offer a new meat offering unto the LORD.

- On the Zadokite Calendar, the seventh and last day of Unleavened Bread (day 21 of the 1st month) is always a weekday 3 (Tuesday). Since they could not attain their wave sheaf prior to that, the next morrow after the weekly Sabbath would be day 26 of the 1st month, a weekday 1 (Sunday). That would be the first possible time for them to wave the sheaf they had reaped, and it matches the Zadokite calendar.

- <u>Our God is a God of patterns</u>. If Father had wanted to pattern the sheaf to be waved during the week of Unleavened Bread, He could have given them the city immediately so they could harvest and wave then, but He did not. <u>This seven-day span of time may well have been partially designed by Father to **prove** that the waving of the first fruits barley sheaf should NOT occur during the week of Unleavened Bread</u> (which He knew would be taught in our day). The Biblical evidence that it COULD NOT have occurred DURING the week of Unleavened Bread in Joshua's day should wake us up.

(Note – Randy's breadcrumbs end here, and we take off on a bit of a tangent of our own as we proceed, so don't blame Randy if what follows is in any way problematic.)

- However, there may be much more to it than that! In fact there had to be a great deal of significance to this elaborate display of marching, blowing of trumpets, and falling of the walls.

- Considering the unspecified timing between the eating of the old grain in Joshua 5:2 and the beginning of the march in 6:7, there is only a slim chance that the march was actually on the exact same seven days as Unleavened Bread. <u>Maybe there was an even more profound reason behind Father's **structural design** of a seven-day march in this passage</u>.

- If there was a slight delay between the eating of the old corn on the 15th day of the 1st month and the receiving of the instructions (which is somewhat likely), then <u>Father might possibly have designed the timing of the marching around the city</u> NOT to coincide with the days of Unleavened Bread, BUT <u>to provide the shadow typing for a VERY significant event</u> in a future era.

- We mustn't fail to note that the Hebrew word for Joshua is likened to the Hebrew name Y'shua.

- <u>The fall of the walls of Jericho represented the Father's giving of the earthly promised land to Joshua.</u> (An extraordinary typology may be unfolding here.)

- Y'shua is to be <u>our High Priest and our King</u> – our priest/king. Before being awarded His position as High Priest, He would have to complete the <u>seven-day consecration period</u> for the priesthood. Once that would conclude, He would be ceremonially ready and in position to be given the title to the Kingdom He will inherit.

- Could it be that the silent lapse of time between the eating of the corn and the beginning of the march corresponded to the time of silence that Y'shua spent in the tomb before His resurrection?

- Might Joshua's seven-day march on earth actually have been designed to parallel <u>the seven-day countdown to the conclusion of the consecration period for Y'shua in Heaven after His resurrection</u>?

- Is it possible that the fall of the walls of Jericho at that precise day and time on the calendar might have been the earthly counterpart depiction of the moment of victory that marked the culmination of all of Y'shua's efforts – the moment when all of His required ceremonial mandates had been completed in order to be deemed our High priest AND be given the title and keys to His Davidic Kingdom?

Revelation 3:7
(7) And to the angel of the church in Philadelphia write; These things saith he that is holy, he that is true, <u>he that hath the key of David</u>, he that openeth, and no man shutteth; and shutteth, and no man openeth;

- In Father's patterning, maybe <u>the earthly promised land was given by the Father to Joshua for his people in the earthly realm</u> in a precise calendar parallel to when <u>the Heavenly promised land was given by the Father to Y'shua for His people in the Heavenly realm</u>. (As is Scripturally common, maybe the earthly was an exact precursor or shadow type of the Heavenly.) When the time was right, maybe <u>Y'shua waved the first fruits sheaf of HIS saints in His new Heavenly promised land on day 26 of the 1st month,</u> <u>just as Joshua waved the first fruits sheaf of his barley in his new earthly promised land on day 26 of the 1st month here.</u>

Wow – what a thrilling picture! When comparing and contrasting the timing for the march and the timing of Unleavened Bread, it just seems to us that there is almost too much activity between Joshua 5:22-6:22 to fit into a single day. First, he ate of the old corn, then he went up to stand by Jericho, then he received the instructions of how to take the city, then he went back to talk to the priests and gather the people and assemble them for the march, then they went back to Jericho and encompassed the city. Whew – that would be quite a day. It seems much more logical that the patterning of the seven-day week of creation might play in here as well, that the first day of the march might have been on weekday one, and the second on weekday two, ending with the seventh being on Sabbath, a day of victory. The priests would then have been easily able to track where they were in the march, as the days would coincide with the weeks they were tracking on the calendar.

On the Zadokite calendar, day one of Unleavened Bread would be on a weekday 4. It seems entirely reasonable that Joshua would have been resting that day – a holy day, after keeping Passover (probably being up all night). Then he stands by Jericho on weekday 5, and is given his marching orders. He returns to speak to the priests and gather the people, and make preparations for the march on weekday 6. They rest on the Sabbath, and then the march begins on weekday 1. The timing from weekday 4 to weekday 1 of the next week would be the exact time Y'shua spent in the tomb, aligning the seven days of the march to the countdown timing for the consecration.

While this is purely speculative on our part, it does seem to fit the patterning of sevens very well. At the very least though, the validation of the waving of the barley sheaf the week after Unleavened Bread is pretty iron-clad. To reiterate and summarize our findings in that respect, we could provide the following thoughts.

Father, in His wisdom, did not put everything in one spot so we could just read it quickly and get it. He wanted us to dig so the answers would be more meaningful. He explains that protocol for finding the meat of His Word in Isaiah 28:10. He has Isaiah disclose that we must be diligent enough to dig out Father's meat Father's way: "For precept must be upon precept, precept upon precept; line upon line, line upon line; here a little, and there a little". If one part of the Word doesn't give us all we need, we need to see what is missing and look to other passages to find it. Then we must pull it all together.

The primary instruction for waving the first fruits barley sheaf is found in Leviticus 23:10, which firmly locks in the timing for it to one specific element – entrance into the land Father will give them: "**When** ye be come into the land **which I give unto you**, and shall reap the harvest thereof, **then** ye shall bring a sheaf of the firstfruits of your harvest unto the priest". So – in order to know the proper timing to offer the sheaf, we must know two things: 1) what land Father was establishing as the "land which I give unto you", and 2) when they entered that specific land. Since these two bits of information are simply not put forth in Leviticus, we have to look to another passage to provide them. We find it neatly packaged for us in the Joshua passage we presented, where he specifically states that 1) Jericho is the land that Father is giving them (6:2), and 2) that the timing for the entry of the land is linked directly and specifically to the Passover time frame by the eating of the old corn the day after Passover (5:11). This Passover reference is then directly followed by their entry into Jericho.

By linking these two passages together, we can easily see that the march would almost assuredly begin within a few days of Passover. Then they would enter the land seven days later when the walls fell. Then they could reap the harvest, and complete the mandate to offer the sheaf of the spring barley harvest to Father that they had been instructed to perform in Leviticus.

Now that we have the Dead Sea Scrolls to specify the timing of the first fruits barley sheaf offering as being day 26 of the 1st month, we can see where it is a hand-in-glove fit with the Scriptural passages of Leviticus 23 and Joshua 5 - 6.

It is only when we combine these two passages that the Scriptural timing for the waving of the sheaf is given the Scriptural context to show when the mandate would have been accomplished. We simply can't get to the fulfillment of the Leviticus instructions without the information we find in Joshua. Only when these two passages overlay one another does the performing of the offering come into its proper perspective.

But What About the Timing for Passover on this Calendar?

Another important understanding from the Hebrew Roots perspective that seems to present an issue here is the crucifixion of Y'shua as our Passover lamb on the 14th day of the 1st month, which occurred on Wednesday. This is in direct conflict with the Zadokite calendar where the 14th day of the 1st month is always on a weekday 3 (Tuesday), a day too early. This very fact alone was initially the specific criterion that caused us to reject this Sabbath-based calendar. Then some research just happened to pop up during our Passover observance on our lunar-based calendar that actually provided a very solid explanation. Thereby the perceived conflict of a Tuesday Passover with a Wednesday crucifixion became our single most defining reason to abandon our loyalty to the lunar system we had ardently supported. In other words, the very reason we could not accept the Sabbath-based Zadokite calendar became a conclusive reason to actually make the changeover to our own personal observance of it.

We know that Y'shua had to fulfill 3 full days and nights in the grave. Otherwise He would not have been so explicit in stating that it would be as the time Jonah was in the whale. His words were as follows:

66

Matthew 12:39-40
(39) But he answered and said unto them, An evil and adulterous generation seeketh after a sign; and there shall no sign be given to it, but the sign of the prophet Jonas:
(40) For as Jonas was three days **and** three nights in the whale's belly; so shall the Son of man be three days **and** three nights in the heart of the earth.

No, Y'shua did not lie, and yes, He meant what He said, "three days AND three nights". Other references seem to lock down the timing of this. The crucifixion could not be before Wednesday or after Wednesday to fulfill all of the mandates of the events recorded in Scripture. It had to occur ON Wednesday.

So, if Y'shua had to be slain on Passover as our Pascal lamb, how does the rendering of Tuesday on the Zadokite calendar work as Passover? Let's look at a passage in Mark that has presented a great deal of confusion over the years:

Mark 14:12-18
(12) And the first day of unleavened bread, **when they killed the passover**, his disciples said unto him, Where wilt thou that we go and prepare that thou mayest **eat the passover**?
(13) And he sendeth forth two of his disciples, and saith unto them, Go ye into the city, and there shall meet you a man bearing a pitcher of water: follow him.
(14) And wheresoever he shall go in, say ye to the goodman of the house, The Master saith, Where is the guestchamber, where I shall eat the passover with my disciples?
(15) And he will shew you a large upper room furnished and prepared: there make ready for us.
(16) And his disciples went forth, and came into the city, and found as he had said unto them: and they made ready the passover.
(17) And in the evening he cometh with the twelve.
(18) And as they sat and **did eat**, Jesus said, Verily I say unto you, One of you which eateth with me shall betray me.

The Bible seems to use the terms "Passover" and "Unleavened Bread" interchangeably to designate the entirety of the spring festivities – extending from Passover THROUGH the week of Unleavened Bread. We know by the context here that "the "first day of unleavened bread" in verse 12 actually indicated the 1st day of these spring festivities, which was actually Passover day - the 14th day of the 1st month. It had to be Passover day because the text specifies that it was the day "**when they killed the Passover**". The Lamb had to be slain the day before the Feast of Unleavened Bread began - on Passover day, the 14th day of the 1st month (the month of Abib):

Exodus 12:6
(6) And ye shall keep it up until the fourteenth day of the same month: and the whole assembly of the congregation of Israel shall kill it in the evening.

If Y'shua was our Passover Lamb (the same lamb that was to be slain on the 14th day of the month), then how is it that He was able to eat the Passover dinner with His disciples later that evening when He should be in the tomb? It seems that theologians don't know quite what to do with this passage! They simply dance around it and "write it off" in various ways, but they don't know how to deal with it in a straightforward manner at all.

There is an explanation that pulls all of this together, but those who have their feet firmly planted in the lunar calendar system may not appreciate it. To piece it together, lets view the rest of the wording in this passage. They were to follow a <u>man carrying a pitcher of water</u> and they were to ask the "<u>goodman of the house</u>" where they might partake of the Passover.

Many sources corroborate that the Essenes were considered to be a sect that was set apart in their aspirations toward holiness, and they are commonly referred to as "goodmen". Carrying water was rarely done by men in the days of Y'shua. It was a task for women and children. However, it is also duly noted that many of the Essenes practiced celebacy. As a result, there were few women and children in their number and it meant that the men frequently had to tend to this task themselves. Thus, it is that Y'shua would have told his disciples to find the man carrying water (an Essene), and have him direct them to the goodman (Essene) of the house.

In an article posted by Israel Institute of Biblical Studies, the upper room was thought to be in the Essene quarter of the city of Jerusalem:

Israel Institute of Biblical Studies - http://jewishstudies.eteacherbiblical.com/upper-room-part-two-judith-green-jonathan-lipnick-hebrew-university-jerusalem/ -
It is said that Caiaphas lived in the Essene quarters close to the Temple, also that the upper room was the place where the Last Supper had taken place.

Such a quarter is verified as well in the excellent study on the Qumran community by Philip R. Davies, George J Brooke, and Phillip R Callaway. They make the following statement:

<u>The Complete World of the Dead Sea Scrolls</u> - by Philip R. Davies, George J Brooke, and Phillip R Callaway - p. 58 -
Josephus never associates the Essenes with a specific location like Qumran, but says that they settled throughout Palestine. He elsewhere mentions an 'Essene gate' on the south side of Jerusalem, which has recently been discovered, and which is generally thought to have belonged to an 'Essene quarter' in that city.

In a segment regarding Jerusalem, the 1906 <u>Jewish Encyclopedia</u> mentions this gate as well:

<u>The 1906 Jewish Encyclopedia</u> - Jewish Encyclopedia.com (the unedited full text of the 1906 Jewish Encyclopedia) - http://www.jewishencyclopedia.com/articles/15265-zion -
The southern-most wall encompassed the upper and the lower city and Ophel. It started at Hippicus, ran south to <u>the Gate of the Essenes at the southwest corner of the city</u>, then east, curving as it approached the Kidron Valley, from which it ran north-northeast, joining the Temple enclosure at its southeastern extremity.

We notice in verse 15 that this room had already been "prepared" for Passover observance.

Mark 14:15 -
(15) And he will shew you a large upper room furnished and <u>prepared</u>: there make ready for us.

Torah says that such preparation consists of removing all leaven from the premises in advance of the arrival of Passover. This had already been done because the Essenes were on the same calendar Y'shua was observing, and it was already the 14th day of the month on this calendar, one day earlier than on the standard calendar.

Davies, Brooke, and Callaway assert that different calendars were in use at the time of Y'shua in the second Temple period:

The Complete World of the Dead Sea Scrolls - by Philip R. Davies, George J Brooke, and Phillip R Callaway
- p 46 –
... the Temple Scroll (p 156) ... describes a different liturgical cycle, and many of the scrolls, a different calendar ... .

We would also note in verse 12 that the disciples asked Y'shua where they could go to "eat the Passover", expressing absolutely no doubt or confusion regarding their timing for their Passover observance. This points to the conclusion that they fully understood the calendar which they and Y'shua observed was a day ahead of the calendar the Temple system was observing in that particular year. If indeed the Essenes were following what we now see as the Zadokite calendar, it would not have matched the Rabbinical version. Historical documentation shows that there were actually multiple calendars in use, and the evidence is very compelling that Y'shua and His disciples were observing the Zadokite version.

The phrase to "eat the Passover" clearly indicates that this would have been the actual Passover meal that was to be observed annually on the evening that ended the 14th, after the slaying of the Pascal lamb. It was not a separate supper, the evening before Passover that some theologians write off merely as "the last supper". A careful reading of Mark 14 shows conclusively that it was their actual Passover meal **at the conclusion of Passover** on the calendar that Y'shua and His disciples were using.

Exodus 12:6-8
(6) And ye shall keep it up until **the fourteenth day of the same month**: and the whole assembly of the congregation of Israel **shall kill it in** the evening.
(7) And they shall take of the blood, and strike it on the two side posts and on the upper door post of the houses, wherein they shall eat it.
(8) **And they shall eat the flesh in that night**, roast with fire, and unleavened bread; and with bitter herbs they shall eat it.

Mark 14:17-18
(17) And **in the evening** he cometh with the twelve.
(18) And as **they sat and did eat**, Jesus said, Verily I say unto you, One of you which eateth with me shall betray me.

Y'shua and his disciples were almost assuredly observing the 364-day solar-based calendar of the Zadokite priesthood and the Essene people. That is NOT to say that Y'shua was a practicing Essene! However, their lifestyles had much in common with that of Y'shua, as well as with John the Baptist, who dwelt in the desert. At the very least, Y'shua seems to have had somewhat of an affinity to the Essene people of His day, and this passage of Mark and associated textual clues seems to indicate that He was observing the same calendar they used! Indeed, it may be the ONLY way to make sense of the timing presented in this passage!

Y'shua and John the Baptist were both very outspoken in their criticism of the Sadducees and the Pharisees - those who dictated the Temple calendar system. Their praise for both was notably absent, and their disdain for them became rather obvious:

Matthew 3:7
(7) But when he saw many of the Pharisees and Sadducees come to his baptism, he said unto them, O generation of vipers, who hath warned you to flee from the wrath to come?

Matthew 12:34

(34) O generation of vipers, how can ye, being evil, speak good things? for out of the abundance of the heart the mouth speaketh.

Matthew 23:25

(25) Woe unto you, scribes and Pharisees, hypocrites! for ye make clean the outside of the cup and of the platter, but within they are full of extortion and excess.

Matthew 16:6, 11-12

(6) Then Jesus said unto them, Take heed and beware of the leaven of the Pharisees and of the Sadducees.

(11) How is it that ye do not understand that I spake it not to you concerning bread, that ye should **beware of the leaven of the Pharisees and of the Sadducees**?

(12) Then understood they how that he bade them not beware of the leaven of bread, but of **the doctrine of the Pharisees and of the Sadducees**.

Could this doctrinal leaven have related (at least partially) to the Temple calendar system that placed all of Father's holy days on the wrong days?

Josephus wrote of the Essenes in Y'shua's day:

The Works of Josephus Complete and Unabridged - Translated by William Whiston, A.M. – The Wars of the Jews – 2.8.2 – p. 605 -

For there are three philosophical sects among the Jews. The followers of the first of whom are the Pharisees; of the second the Sadducees; and the third sect, who pretends to a severer discipline, and called Essenes. These last are Jews by birth, and seem to have a greater affection for one another than the other sects have. ... These Essenes reject pleasures as an evil, but esteem continence, and the conquest over our passions, to be virtue. ... .

So, we see that the Essene sect was the third philosophical faction of Y'shua's day. Though the Essene faction is never specifically mentioned in the Word, we have seen that it is implied. It was a very real and vibrant sect of Believers in Y'shua's day, and unlike the other two major religious sects at that time, Y'shua never condemned it.

Because their Zadokite calendar always begins on a weekday 4 (Wednesday) after the Equinox, the 1st day of the 1st month would be on this day. The 14th day of that month then would always be on a weekday 3 (Tuesday). On the lunar-based Temple calendar system on the year of Y'shua's crucifixion, the 14th would have been on a weekday 4 (Wednesday). Y'shua observed the Passover dinner on a weekday 3 (Tuesday) by receiving the cup from Father to drink for the atonement of mankind. Drinking this cup started and sealed the death process. He proclaimed His role as He partook of the elements that Passover evening of the Zadokite calendar with His disciples:

Mark 14:24-25

(24) And he said unto them, This is my blood of the new testament, which is shed for many.

(25) Verily I say unto you, I will drink no more of the fruit of the vine, until that day that I drink it new in the kingdom of God.

It was at this time (after Judus had received the sop and left them) that Y'shua was glorified and the Father was glorified in Him:

John 13:31
(31) Therefore, when he was gone out, Jesus said, Now is the Son of man glorified, and God is glorified in him.

Y'shua had drunk from the Father's cup and the process of His death and resurrection had begun. He would later question if there was another way - could His drinking of the cup somehow be reversed:

Luke 22:42-44
(42) Saying, Father, if thou be willing, **remove** this cup from me: nevertheless not my will, but thine, be done.
(43) And there appeared an angel unto him from heaven, strengthening him.
(44) And being in an agony he prayed more earnestly: and his sweat was as it were great drops of blood falling down to the ground.

He was not asking to avoid having to drink from the cup of the Father, but that the cup He had already received might be <u>removed</u>.

His proclamation of the wine being His blood, and the bread being His body was declaration of His role as the Passover Lamb. This pronouncement on the 14th of the Zadokite calendar, and His sharing the elements with His disciples at that time substantiates that the solemn and deliberate process of His Sacrifice had begun on the correct day.

He then progressed through the passion on a weekday 4 (Wednesday), and concluded the process on the 14th day of the Temple system calendar, during the "Passover of the Jews" at the same time their Passover lambs were being slain. In this way, the Jews who were under the Temple system calendar would be able to clearly identify Y'shua as their Pascal lamb one day. It was then that He gave up the ghost:

Luke 23:46
(46) And when Jesus had cried with a loud voice, he said, Father, into thy hands I commend my spirit: and having said thus, he gave up the ghost.

CHAPTER 16

SUDDEN UNEXPECTED VALIDATION

As this book was about to go into publication, an article came to our attention. Two Dead Sea Scrolls had initially been set aside due to their encrypted Hebrew format, and also because many tiny fragments of the scroll (some only 1 square centimeter in size) needed to be pieced together. Other scrolls were given priority so the work could proceed on a more timely basis. At last though, aided by digital technology, Dr. Eshbal Ratson from the Department of Bible Studies at the University of Haifa took up the challenge and tackled Scroll 4Q324d. She was supervised by Professor Jonathan Ben-Dove, head of the Haifa Project for Research on the Dead Sea Scrolls. This scroll employed a "Cryptic A script" technique, which was a replacement code type of encryption. Each letter was replaced by a designated sign. Paleo-Hebrew letters were employed as some of these signs, while others seemed more arbitrary. Breaking the code was only the beginning of the project though, as piecing together the tiny fragments was a particularly arduous task.

After about a year of very challenging endeavors, Dr. Ratson completed the intricate exercise of successfully and unequivocally piecing together the 60 fragments and deciphering the coded message in scroll 4Q324d, the first of these two final scrolls. Her article, A Newly Reconstructed Calendrical Scroll from Qumran in Cryptic Script, detailed her preliminary conclusions. It was co-authored by Professor Ben Dov, and was published in the Journal of Biblical Literature (Volume 136, No. 4, Winter 2017, pp 905-936).
Her findings took the world by storm. The articles that have been published by various prestigious news sources since its release are numerous. Many of these news reports mentioned that the wording and expressions noted in the text of the scroll tied it to the Second Temple era, as it matched the phraseology of the Talmud from the same time period. Dr. Ratson's journal entry and press release has provided overwhelming evidence that the fragments of 4Q324d did, indeed, form a comprehensive calendrical scroll of the Second Temple era. Those who followed this calendar used mathematical computations to established the rhythmical flow of their year, and the delineation of the seasons they observed.

The calendar of Scroll 4Q324d details a symmetrical 364-day system that parallels what we have already put forth. Dr. Ratson described this system as being "perfect" because 364 divides evenly by seven, allowing every special day to fall on the same day of the week and a fixed date each year. This anomaly prevents any holy day from overlying a weekly Sabbath, maintaining a separate and independent observance for each.

Aligning perfectly to the calendar references in other Dead Sea Scrolls, Scroll 4Q324d recorded the consistent addition of a 31st day (an epogomenal, or intercalary day - which we have called a day out of time) to the end of the third month of each season. Work on previous scrolls had evidenced these special days, but until this text was deciphered, there had not been a word in any scroll to identify them. This scroll revealed that the name for the intercalary day added each quarter was "tekufah". This intercalary "tekafah" day joined the last day of the old seasonal quarter to the first day of the new. The seasons were foundational for the holy days decreed by God, as the timing of His holy days are basically agricultural in nature. The year always begins on the 4th day of the week, the day the heavenly bodies were created, which made it possible for the counting of time to begin on that day. By using 91-day intervals (exactly 13 weeks) for every seasonal transition, the calendar of Scroll 4Q324d assured that every season would likewise begin on a fourth day of the week. The "tekufah" days are always on a Tuesday, which keeps the first day of the new season on Wednesday, without exception.

Recall from our research that the Hebrew word for "end" in Exodus 34:22 and "circuit" in Psalms 19:6 was Strong's H8622, which describes the circuit or passage of the sun across the sky. It is phonetically transliterated as "tĕquwphah". The word "tekufah" used in Scroll 4Q324d would be the same word, which validates the concept of the "chodesh" aspect - the transition from old to new. The course of the sun from one equinox or solstice event to the next would apply directly to the "tekufah" as it was used in this scroll, and each "tekufah" would almost certainly have been the point of transition for that specific "chodesh" event. The word "tekufah" had never been found in any Dead Sea scrolls prior to its discovery in 4Q324d, so some think of it as a "new" word. Yet the Israeli news source *Haaretz*, reported Dr. Ratson's acknowledgement that the "tekufah" concept is actually from very early in the religious Jewish law ("halakha").

The calendar that emerged from Scroll 4Q324d adds information about other feasts as well. One such feast is the feast of wood offering, which is observed for six days at the end of the year. Further specifics about its observance are not provided, but it is thought to be in accordance with Nehemiah 13:31:

Nehemiah 13:31
(31) And for the wood offering, at times appointed, and for the firstfruits. Remember me, O my God, for good.

Other festivals were mentioned as well – the festival of new wine and the festival of new oil. These festivals were extensions of the festival of Shavuot, which is a festival that features wheat. Each progressive festival provides a 50-day divider in the course of the calendar. Some of the most comprehensive reporting on scroll 4Q324d was by the Jewish Press. It was published on January 21, 2018, and it tells of the wine and oil festivals.

Reconstructed, Deciphered, Throwing Light on Alternative Jewish Calendar -
http://www.jewishpress.com/news/israel/one-of-last-two-qumran-scrolls-reconstructed-deciphered-throwing-light-on-alternative-jewish-calendar/2018/01/21/ -
... the wheat festival took place 50 days after the Shabbat that followed Passover, then, 50 days later, came the wine harvest festival, and another 50 days later the oil harvest festival.

This would be another example of the term "Passover" designating the entirety of the spring festivities – extending from Passover THROUGH the week of Unleavened Bread. It is obvious from our other scroll deductions that this calendar rendered the Shabbat (or Sabbath) "that followed Passover" as being on the 25th day of the first month, after the entire festival had concluded. The day following then began the 50 day count to Shavuot when the wheat festival was acknowledged.

So - the new barley is featured as the offering in the first month of the year. Then 50 days later, the new wheat is offered at Shavuot. Scroll 4Q324d then suggests that the offering of new wine is offered 50 days after Shavuot, then the new oil is offered 50 days after the festival of new wine. This extended festival activity then spans from the waving of barley first fruits sheaf in the first month (spring) of the calendar through the next five months, leaving only a few days until the autumnal equinox and the beginning of the fall season. Though there is no specific verse in the Bible that speaks of the festivals of new wine or new oil, there is a reference in the book of Numbers that might indicate the first fruits offering of wine and oil at their respective harvests, just as the first fruits of barley and wheat are offered at their respective harvests.

Numbers 18:12
(12) All the best of the oil, and all the best of the wine, and of the wheat, the firstfruits of them which they shall offer unto the LORD, them have I given thee.

Along with these actual calendrical findings, the researchers also point to the strife and struggle that had ensued between those who followed the calendar of Scroll 4Q324d and the ruling rabbinic priesthood that mandated calendar decisions in Second Temple days.

Paraphrasing yet more of the reporting in the aforementioned article by Jewish Press, we see that the rabbinic calendar was based on the cycles of the moon and had to be adjusted to fit the solar year. This was done by implementing a 19-year cycle, whereby an extra lunar month was included in their leap years. We know this to be true yet today.

It seems that those who followed the scroll 4Q324d calendar simply could not accept the man-made authority they associated with the current priesthood's version of the luni-solar calendar. Abiding by the lunar aspects of this calendar requires a lot of human decisions; along with observation of the moon, human assessment was needed to determine when to implement a leap year by adding an extra month before the new year could begin.

Conversely, when using the Qumran version, the transition from one year to the next was easily and neatly determined by a single heavenly event, and the months evolved naturally from that point. Because the flow of this calendar prevented the holy days from ever falling on the weekly Sabbath, there was no need to decide what to do about such an occurrence, which was a troubling enigma with the lunar calendar. Nothing was left to man's discretion; it was all perfectly predicated by God's majestic handiwork, and His heavenly display gave man the needed concrete information to chart his course. The adherents to the scroll calendar believed that the design of God's heavenly provision was perfect, and intervention by man was to be rejected, so they steadfastly followed the calendar they believed God had provided for them thousands of years before.

Drawing on this perspective, in a related discussion, researcher and published author, Bodie Hodge also cited the Babylonian nature of the lunar calendar. He notes that the months on this calendar are named after Babylonian gods; citing that the month of Tammuz correlates to the Babylonian god Tammuz, etc.

Carrying this thought through, it would be obvious that the people who followed the 4Q324d calendar (being purists by nature), would find such names abhorrent, and they would see the displacement of God's holy days on such a calendar as mixing the holy with the profane in various respects. As well as believing that the holy days on the lunar calendar were actually on the wrong dates, their aversion to both the role of man's subjective discernment and the Babylonian influence would have made the lunar calendar of their day abominable to them. Rebellion toward the use of the calendar decreed by the ruling rabbinic authority then makes a great deal of sense. The researchers concur; the press release by Dr. Ratson and Professor Ben Dov concluded that the steadfast and unchanging nature of the ancient 4Q324d calendar corresponds to the perfection and holiness of this people.

In more exciting news, it was revealed that Dr. Ratson has now begun work on the second of the two scrolls in "Cryptic A" format. It is a calendrical astronomical scroll. If the time frame is the same as the first one, maybe in another year or so we'll have even more information to draw together!

Another new revelation to us is a recent development in Jerusalem. Near the Old City and David's Citadel, across from the Jaffa Gate, travelers to Jerusalem can visit Kollek Park. The park was established by the Jerusalem Foundation, and named for Jerusalem's long-serving mayor Teddy Kollek.

Established by Mayor Kollek in 1966, the Jerusalem Foundation is a nonprofit foundation that is dedicated to many avenues of social and cultural endeavors, including restoration of ancient sites and the sponsoring of archeological excavations and other venues of cultural interests. One of their projects became the formation of Kollek Park. As the construction for the park ensued, the foundation commissioned a renowned sculptor, Maty Grunberg to construct a sundial as a major attraction.

Maty Grunberg of Skopie, Macedonia had immigrated to Israel in 1948 where he finished his studies "with honors" at "Bezalel Academy of Art" in Jerusalem, and then completed his M. A. at "Central School of Art and Design" in London in 1971. He had returned to Israel in 2007 and opened a studio in Bat-Yam. Utilizing the scientific expertise of astronomer Ilan Manulis (director of the Martin S Kraar Observatory, Department of Particle Physics and Astrophysics, Weizmann Institute of Science, Rehovot Israel) and sundial designer Dr. Valentin Hristov of Bulgaria, Maty Grunberg planned and designed a magnificent stone sundial for public viewing.

The purpose of this sundial is to follow the cyclical movement of the sun as it crosses the sky throughout the year. This sundial is precisely calibrated to its specific location, and it accurately delineates both equinox and solstice timing in Jerusalem.

Kollek Park was only recently opened in 2013. Why did the Jerusalem Foundation commission Maty Grunberg's construction of a sundial? There has been (to our knowledge) no reason given. However, they were somehow inspired to do so. It seems to us to be no coincidence that Father would prompt the motivation to bring about such an observable timing element as this fabulous sundial in the city where He has put His name (1 Kings 14:21). We had been convicted of the necessity to make all of our timing calculations for the Zadokite calendar from Jerusalem's perspective long before we found that this sundial was now displayed there. How very fitting that the apple (pupil) of God's eye (Zechariah 2:2 & 8) is the very place where Father seems to have orchestrated the placement of such a timing mechanism for man's use at this particular time – the same point in time that people are starting to see what the Dead Sea Scrolls reveal about His calendar.

CHAPTER 17

THE CHALLENGE

Well, we had come to develop considerable confidence in the lunar calendar system we had previously researched. Now, we had to determine what we, personally, were going to do about our new findings. To change at this point meant that there would be very few who would be in agreement with us. This meant that once again we'd be swimming against the current, only now it was concerning our Hebrew Roots fellowship! However, we had to face a very important question. Should compliance with man or acceptability by man be more important than our commitment to meet with Father on the Holy Days that we had come to understand He meant?

Why Not Do as Y'shua Did?

If indeed Y'shua abided by the Zadokite calendar system rather than the Temple's version, why do we today honor the Temple's calendar version rather than the Zadokite version?

It is obvious as we review several Old Testament mandates that sacrifices were to be presented not only on Sabbaths and feast days, but also on "chodesh" days. We will provide five such examples, but we will be reverting to the language of the original manuscripts in place of the questionable English translation of "new moons".

1 Chronicles 23:31
(31) And to offer all <u>burnt sacrifices</u> unto the LORD in the sabbaths, in the [chodeshim], and on the set feasts, by number, according to the order commanded unto them, continually before the LORD:

2 Chronicles 2:4
(4) Behold, I build an house to the name of the LORD my God, to dedicate it to him, and to burn before him sweet incense, and for the continual shewbread, and for the <u>burnt offerings</u> morning and evening, on the sabbaths, and on the [chodeshim], and on the solemn feasts of the LORD our God. This is an ordinance for ever to Israel.

2 Chronicles 8:13
(13) Even after a certain rate every day, <u>offering</u> according to the commandment of Moses, on the sabbaths, and on the [chodeshim], and on the solemn feasts, three times in the year, even in the feast of unleavened bread, and in the feast of weeks, and in the feast of tabernacles.

2 Chronicles 31:3
(3) He appointed also the king's portion of his substance for the burnt offerings, to wit, for the morning and evening burnt offerings, and the <u>burnt offerings</u> for the sabbaths, and for the [chodeshim], and for the set feasts, as it is written in the law of the LORD.

Nehemiah 10:33
(33) For the shewbread, and for the continual meat offering, and for the continual burnt offering, of the sabbaths, of the [chodeshim], for the set feasts, and for the holy things, and for the sin offerings to make an atonement for Israel, and for all the work of the house of our God.

What if these "chodeshim" are indeed seasonal transition days as reckoned by the Zadokite calendar instead of "new moon" days? The scrolls support the concept of offerings being made on these festive occasions. We don't burn sacrifices today, but these verses illustrate that perhaps these "chodesh" days hold a significant relevance to Father, just as His appointed weekly Sabbaths and the high holy days of the feasts. Obviously, they would not be properly honored if we are using the lunar calendar system. Furthermore, if we are using the wrong calendar system, then even Father's solemn feast days (as they are Biblically stated in Leviticus 23) are not being honored at their proper times. Could this have something to do with the prophetic vision of Isaiah and Yahweh's condemnation recorded by the prophet Ezekiel? They are very troubling:

Isaiah 1:13-14
(13) Bring no more vain oblations; incense is an abomination unto me; the new moons and sabbaths, the calling of assemblies, I cannot away with; **it is iniquity, even the solemn meeting**.
(14) **Your** new moons and **your** appointed feasts my soul hateth: they are a trouble unto me; I am weary to bear them.

Ezekiel 22:26
(26) Her priests have violated **my** law, and have profaned **mine** holy things: they have put no difference between the holy and profane, neither have they shewed difference between the unclean and the clean, and have hid their eyes from **my** sabbaths, and I am profaned among them.

Could these Biblical passages relate to the admonition found in The Book of the Jubilees which tells of the Zadokite calendar? Could there be a connection? The Hebrew word for "new moons" in both verses of Isaiah 1 is "chodeshim". Why would their observation of "chodeshim" and feast days be offensive to Yahweh? If the solemn meeting of Isaiah 1:13 was Day of Atonement, and it was being observed on the wrong day, might this have bearing on Ezekiel's words regarding the difference between the holy and the profane, and the difference between the unclean and the clean? Here is some similar wording, the prophetic statement of The Book of Jubilees:

The Book of Jubilees 6:36-37 - The Researchers Library of Ancient Texts Volume 1 - by R.H. Charles, Oxford – p. 289 -
*...there will be those who will assuredly make observations of the moon -how (it) disturbs the seasons and comes in from year to year ten days too soon. For this reason the years will come upon them when they will disturb (the order), and make an abominable (day) **the day of testimony**, and an **unclean day** a feast day, and they will confound all the days, **the holy with the unclean, and the unclean day with the holy**; for they will go wrong as to the months and sabbaths and feasts and jubilees.*

The "day of testimony" in this passage is almost assuredly the Day of Atonement, the holiest day of the year to Father, when we are to afflict our souls. If we are using the wrong calendar, this somber day could fall on the first day of the Feast of Tabernacles. Then instead of introspection, confession, and affliction, we would be spending that day in celebration. We would actually be feasting on the day we should be fasting.

Other passages from the Bible echo these concerns:

Malachi 2:3
(3) Behold, I will corrupt your seed, and spread dung upon your faces, even <u>the dung of your solemn feasts</u>; and one shall take you away with it.

Malachi 2:8-9
(8) But ye are departed out of the way; ye have caused many to stumble at the law; **ye have corrupted the covenant of Levi**, saith the LORD of hosts.
(9) Therefore have I also made you contemptible and base before all the people, according as **ye have not kept my ways**, but have been partial in the law.

Malachi 2:11-12
(11) <u>Judah hath dealt treacherously, and an abomination is committed in Israel and in Jerusalem; for Judah hath profaned the holiness of the LORD</u> which he loved, **and hath married the daughter of a strange god**.
(12) The LORD will cut off the man that doeth this, the master and the scholar, out of the tabernacles of Jacob, and him that offereth an offering unto the LORD of hosts.

Hosea 5:1-7
(1) Hear ye this, O priests; and hearken, ye house of Israel; and give ye ear, O house of the king; for judgment is toward you, because ye have been a snare on Mizpah, and a net spread upon Tabor.
(2) And the revolters are profound to make slaughter, though I have been a rebuker of them all.
(3) I know Ephraim, and Israel is not hid from me: for now, O Ephraim, thou committest whoredom, and Israel is defiled.
(4) They will not frame their doings to turn unto their God: for the spirit of whoredoms is in the midst of them, and they have not known the LORD.
(5) And the pride of Israel doth testify to his face: therefore shall Israel and Ephraim fall in their iniquity; Judah also shall fall with them.
(6) They shall go with their flocks and with their herds to seek the LORD; but they shall not find him; he hath withdrawn himself from them.
(7) <u>They have dealt treacherously against the LORD: for they have begotten strange children: now shall a month devour them with their portions.</u>

There seems to be no link in the literal natural understanding between "begotten strange children" and the means by which a "month" shall "devour them with their portions". This is by all accounts a spiritual application, and a pronouncement by Yahweh of His displeasure. Maybe it is time to come to terms with this warning, and to take it seriously!

It is interesting that the word "month" in verse 7 is "chodesh". It is very strange wording. If the "chodeshim" are on the wrong dates, it could be responsible for some very adverse events. The word "devour" is Strong's H398 ('akal) – *eat, consume, destroy*. The word "portions" is Strong's H2506 (cheleq) - *smoothness, seductiveness, flatteries*. If indeed the ways of the heathen are accepted, this would apply nicely. This might be viewing how lunar "chodesh" observances would bring judgment upon such seduction.

Have we been seduced into marrying "the daughter of a strange god" by adopting heathen practices and subsequently begetting 'strange children' by observing lunar months which puts Yahweh's holy feast days on the wrong dates?

Now we are not saying that all of the condemning words of the prophets above relate exclusively to calendar timing issues. However, it may have contributed to Father's frustrations, and the Bible DOES tell us to abstain from the ways of the heathen:

Jeremiah 10:2
(2) Thus saith the LORD, Learn not **the way of the heathen**, and be not **dismayed at the signs of heaven**; for the heathen are dismayed at them.

This latter passage specifically links heathen practice with the signs of the heaven.

The Hebrew word "dismayed" in this verse is Strong's H2865 (chathath) and can mean: *to be shattered, be broken.*

The Hebrew word "signs" is Strong's H226 ('owth) - *signs and signals.*
It seems to indicate that the WAY in which the heathen were observing the signs of the heavens was destructive to them (brought them under condemnation?). The Hebrew people are cautioned here not to observe the signs of heaven in the WAY or manner of the heathen.

We'll refresh a quote from above for your reference again:

The 1906 Jewish Encyclopedia - Jewish Encyclopedia.com (the unedited full text of the 1906 Jewish Encyclopedia) -http://www.jewishencyclopedia.com/articles/3920-calendar-history-of -
*The **Babylonian years were soli-lunar**; that is to say, the year of 12 months containing **354 days** was bound to the solar year of 365 days by intercalating, as occasion required, a thirteenth month. Out of every 11 years there were 7 with 12 months and 4 with 13 months. ... The Talmud (Yerushalmi, Rosh ha-Shanah i. 1) correctly states that **the Jews got the names of the months at the time of the Babylonian exile.***

In a refreshingly positive passage, Ezekiel prophesies of a Temple in the new Millennial Kingdom:

Ezekiel 44:15
(15) But the priests the Levites, **the sons of Zadok**, that **kept the charge of my sanctuary when the children of Israel went astray from me**, they shall come near to me to minister unto me, and **they shall stand before me** to offer unto me the fat and the blood, saith the Lord GOD:

It seems like the Dead Sea Scrolls may bring some light to this matter as well. When we look to the Damascus Scroll, we find an entry that may indeed speak to this matter:

Dead Sea Scrolls Translated, Qumran Text in English - by Florentino Garcia Martinez - The Damascus Document – CD III 12-16, p. 35 –
... But with those who remained steadfast in God's precepts, with those who were left from among them, God established his covenant with Israel for ever, revealing to them hidden matters in which all Israel had gone astray: his holy Sabbaths and his glorious feasts, his just stipulations and his truthful paths, and the wishes of his will which man must do in order to live by them. ...

Referring back to a previous quote, we would recall that the "old calendar" (in preference to the one being used by the current priesthood) was a significant part of this steadfastness or faithfulness, and would have been primary in the proper determination of Yahweh's "holy Sabbaths and his glorious feasts":

Understanding the Dead Sea Scrolls: A Reader From the Biblical Archaeology Review - by Hershel Shanks
– p. 80-81 -
*The faithful retreated to the desert to live a life of ritual purity, observing the ancient law, **following the old calendar that marked the holy times**, and awaiting the day when the Teacher of Righteousness would be accepted by all Jews as High Priest and would return once again to Jerusalem.*

It may be that the calendar was front and center to the children of Israel going astray while the Zadokite priesthood remained faithful to His intended calendar.

Yahweh is Not the Author of Confusion

It seems that Yahweh would not want confusion relative to the observance of His calendar, since 1 Corinthians 14:33 adamantly states that He is NOT the author of confusion. Far from being confusing, the Zadokite calendar as it is revealed in the Dead Sea Scrolls is simplistic and direct. Because it is a Sabbath-based calendar with equal weeks, Yahweh's annual holy day Sabbaths will always fall on the same weekdays each year. For this reason, there will never be any need for postponements. Likewise, there would be no subjective visual calls or judgments in its formation. Yahweh's annual holy day Sabbaths will ALWAYS fall on exactly the right days of the week as well as the right days of the months and years. There is not even any need for instruction per se. This calendar is so simple a third grader can navigate it with ease. One will simply begin each new year at the weekday 4 after the vernal equinox, and let the rest unfold naturally for the remainder of the year. It will proceed with 30-day months each month, though completing each quarter at the end of its 3rd month with the insertion of an intercalary day - i.e. 30, 30, 31; 30, 30, 31; 30, 30, 31; and 30, 30, 31. The only need for humans to consult any of the signs in the sky is simply to determine the vernal equinox each year.

Considering Enoch

Another text seems to concur with this calendar system, and actually serves to clarify it a bit more. The Book of Enoch covers this entire process in considerable detail. The New World Encyclopedia informs us that the dating of the currently known texts of this book are from the time of the Maccabeans (about 160 BC). They categorize this book as an "apocraphal and pseudopigraphal collection of second century Jewish texts". They acknowledge that Christendom at large does not view the work as canon, but they do inform us that the Ethiopian Orthodox Church does regard at least portions of the work to be inspired Scripture.

Just as manuscript fragments from every book of our Bible except Esther have been found in the Dead Sea Scrolls of Qumran, likewise were various writings within The Book of Enoch among the findings. The manner in which the movements of the luminaries in the heavens are related in The Book of Enoch is strikingly similar to the pattern shown in The Book of Jubilees as it was related above. For your reference, we will include a rather lengthy quote of the chapter that relates closely to The Book of Jubilees text and the pattern shown above. However, if you don't want to read the entire quote, we have summarized it at the end for you.

The Book of Enoch 72:1-32 - The Researchers Library of Ancient Texts Volume 1 - by R.H. Charles, Oxford
– pp. 32-34 -
The book of the courses of the luminaries of the heaven, the relations of each, according to their classes, their dominion and their seasons, according to their names and places of origin, and according to their months, which Uriel, the holy angel, who was with me, who is their guide, showed me; and he showed me all their laws exactly as they are, and how it is with regard to all the years of the world and unto eternity, till the new creation is accomplished which dureth till eternity. And this is the first law of the luminaries: the luminary

the Sun has its rising in the eastern portals of the heaven, and its setting in the western portals of the heaven. And I saw <u>six portals</u> in which the sun rises, and six portals in which the sun sets and the moon rises and sets in these portals, and the leaders of the stars and those whom they lead: six in the east and six in the west, and all following each other in accurately corresponding order: also many windows to the right and left of these portals. And first there goes forth the great luminary, named the Sun, and his circumference is like the circumference of the heaven, and he is quite filled with illuminating and heating fire. The chariot on which he ascends, the wind drives, and the sun goes down from the heaven and returns through the north in order to reach the east, and is so guided that he comes to the appropriate (lit. 'that') portal and shines in the face of the heaven. In this way he rises <u>in the first month in the great portal, which is the fourth</u> [those six portals in the east]. And in that fourth portal from which the sun rises in the first month are twelve window-openings, from which proceed a flame when they are opened in their season. When the sun rises in the heaven, he comes forth <u>through that fourth portal thirty mornings in succession</u>, and sets accurately in the fourth portal in the west of the heaven. <u>And during this period the day becomes daily longer and the night nightly shorter to the thirtieth morning</u>. On that day the day is longer than the night by a ninth part, and the day amounts exactly to ten parts and the night to eight parts. And the sun rises from that fourth portal, and sets in the fourth and returns to the <u>fifth portal</u> of the east <u>thirty mornings</u>, and rises from it and sets in the fifth portal. And then the day becomes longer by two parts and amounts to eleven parts, and the night becomes shorter and amounts to seven parts. And it returns to the east and enters into the <u>sixth portal</u>, and rises and sets in the sixth portal <u>one-and-thirty mornings</u> on account of its sign. <u>On that day the day becomes longer than the night, and the day becomes double the night, and the day becomes twelve parts, and the night is shortened and becomes six parts</u>. And the sun mounts up to make the day shorter and the night longer, and the sun returns to the east and enters into the <u>sixth portal</u>, and rises from it and sets <u>thirty mornings</u>. And when thirty mornings are accomplished, the day decreases by exactly one part, and becomes eleven parts, and the night seven. And the sun goes forth from that sixth portal in the west, and goes to the east and rises in the <u>fifth portal for thirty mornings</u>, and sets in the west again in the fifth western portal. On that day the day decreases by two parts, and amounts to ten parts and the night to eight parts. And the sun goes forth from that fifth portal and sets in the fifth portal of the west, and rises in the <u>fourth portal for one-and-thirty mornings</u> on account of its sign, and sets in the west. <u>On that day the day is equalized with the night, [and becomes of equal length], and the night amounts to nine parts and the day to nine parts</u>. And the sun rises from that portal and sets in the west, and returns to the east and <u>rises thirty mornings in the third portal</u> and sets in the west in the third portal. And on that day the night becomes longer than the day, and night becomes longer than night, and day shorter than day till the thirtieth morning, and the night amounts exactly to ten parts and the day to eight parts. And the sun rises from that third portal and sets in the third portal in the west and returns to the east, <u>and for thirty mornings rises in the second portal</u> in the east, and in like manner sets in the second portal in the west of the heaven. And on that day the night amounts to eleven parts and the day to seven parts. And the sun rises on that day from that second portal and sets in the west in the second portal, and returns to the east into the <u>first portal for one-and-thirty mornings</u>, and sets in the first portal in the west of the heaven. And <u>on that day the night becomes longer and amounts to the double of the day: and the night amounts exactly to twelve parts and the day to six</u>. And the sun has (therewith) traversed the divisions of his orbit and <u>turns again on those divisions of his orbit, and enters that portal thirty mornings</u> and sets also in the west opposite to it. And on that night has the night decreased in length by a ninth part, and the night has become eleven parts and the day seven parts. And the sun has returned and entered into the <u>second portal</u> in the east, and returns on those his divisions of his orbit <u>for thirty mornings</u>, rising and setting. And on that day the night decreases in length, and the night amounts to ten parts and the day to eight. And on that day the sun rises from that portal, and sets in the west, and returns to the east, and rises in the <u>third portal for one-and-thirty mornings</u>, and sets in the west of the heaven. <u>On that day the night decreases and amounts to nine parts, and the day to nine parts, and the night is equal to the day</u> and <u>the year is exactly as to its days three hundred and sixty-four.</u>

81

The summary of this text would then be as follows:

The sun rises in 6 eastern portals (regions of the sky) during the course of the year, and it sets in the 6 contrasting portals in the western sky. (These pairs of portals are numbered the same. For instance, the 4th portal would be the 4th eastern portal for the rising of the sun, and the 4th western portal for the setting of the sun.) The year begins when the days and nights are equal in length (the vernal equinox in the spring). At this time the sun begins to rise and set in the 4th portal of the eastern and western sky. This continues for 30 days. Then it rises and sets in the 5th portal for another 30 days. It then rises and sets in the 6th portal, but this time, the duration is for 31 days. At the end of this time, the days are the longest they will be all year (about twice the length of the nights). It is the summer solstice. The sun rises and sets in the 6th portal yet again to begin the reverse track. This continues for another 30 days. Then the sun moves back to the 5th portal for 30 days. It then continues back to the 4th portal for 31 days. Another seasonal juncture is marked by this extra day. The days and nights are again equal in length. It is the autumnal equinox. The sun then moves to rise and set in the 3rd portal for 30 days. It moves then to the 2nd for 30 days. Then it rises and sets in the 1st portal for 31 days. As this extra day appears, again the seasonal change is marked. The nights are about twice as long as the days. It is the winter solstice. The sun remains in the 1st portal for another 30 days to reverse course yet again. Then it moves back to the 2nd portal for 30 more days. Finally, it returns to the 3rd portal for 31 days. This concludes the 364-day year. The day and night are again equal in length. It is now the vernal equinox, and it is time for the next year to begin again in the 4th portal.

This clearly shows the 30, 30, 31, 30, 30, 31, 30, 30, 31, 30, 30, 31 pattern we have referenced. Further regarding the 4 intercalary days, The Book of Enoch states that these 4 days are:

The Book of Enoch 75:1 - The Researchers Library of Ancient Texts Volume 1 - by R.H. Charles, Oxford – p. 35 -
...*inseparable from their office, according to the reckoning of the year, and these render service on the four days which are not reckoned in the reckoning of the year.*

"Inseparable from their office" reaffirms the assertion that they must be placed in their correct seasonal designations, and "not reckoned in the reckoning of the year" confirms that these intercalary days are a type of days "out of time". They do not count in the reckoning of the twelve 30-day months in the framework for the base calendar year.

Regarding the sun, this book also states:

The Book of Enoch 75:4 - The Researchers Library of Ancient Texts Volume 1 - by R.H. Charles, Oxford – p. 36 -
*... the rays of the sun break forth: and from them is warmth diffused over the earth, **when they are opened at their appointed seasons***.

The stars are mentioned as well. Enoch draws them together with the sun and moon:

The Book of Enoch 75:7 – The Researchers Library of Ancient Texts Volume 1 - by R.H. Charles, Oxford – p. 36 -
... one window at its (appointed) season produces warmth, corresponding ... to those doors from which the stars come forth according as He has commanded them, and wherein they set corresponding to their number. ... .

In summarizing his instruction regarding the luminaries, the book states:

The Book of Enoch 82:4-5, 7, 9 – The Researchers Library of Ancient Texts Volume 1 - by R.H. Charles, Oxford - pp. 39-40 -
Blessed are all the righteous, blessed are all those <u>who walk in the way of righteousness and sin not as the sinners</u>, <u>in the reckoning of all their days</u> *in which the sun traverses the heaven, entering into and departing from the portals for* **thirty days** *with the heads of thousands of the order of the stars,* **together with the four which are intercalated which divide the four portions of the year**, *which lead them and enter with them four days.* <u>Owing to them men shall be at fault and not reckon them in the whole reckoning of the year: yea men shall be at fault and not recognize them accurately.</u> *... And the account thereof is accurate and the recorded reckoning thereof exact; for the luminaries and months and festivals, and years and days, has Uriel shown and revealed to me, to whom the Lord of the whole creation of the world hath subjected the host of heaven. ... And these are the orders of the stars, which set in their places, and in their* <u>seasons and festivals and months</u>.

This first and last portions of text are troubling, as was that which we read in <u>The Book of Jubilees</u>. Men will be found to be at fault for not reckoning the year accurately. It will affect the timing of the festivals which Yahweh ordained so we could meet with Him at the very specific times He designated! It implies that this may actually even have bearing on whether we are seen as walking in righteousness or sin. Though this entire calendar option has been hidden for some time, Father has opened it up to us in our current day. The question then becomes, what do we do with it? Do we look to it as our calendar source and the determining factor for dating Yahweh's appointed festival days, or do we look the other way and continue to use the Hillel calendar provided by the Rabbinical priesthood of our day as our guide to the appropriate times to meet with Yahweh?

CHAPTER 18

ARE WE OBLIGATED TO ADHERE TO PRIESTLY RULING?

There is a common teaching that seemed at first to be troubling. It brought into question whether or not we have the liberty to keep the calendar we feel is right. Was there a mandatory calendar that we must observe to be Biblically compliant? We needed to study it out, and we did.

The Pharisees of our Day – Do We Honor Their Instruction?

A major argument today suggests that we are Biblically obliged to adhere to the Hillel calendar provided by the Rabbinic authority. This is primarily drawn from Matthew:

Matthew 23:2-3
(2) Saying, The scribes and the Pharisees sit in Moses' seat:
(3) All therefore whatsoever **they** bid you observe, that observe and do; but do not ye after their works: for they say, and do not.

In reference to "the scribes and the Pharisees" of verse 2, we find in Ellicott's Commentary for English Readers: "The words were probably spoken of their collective action as represented in the Sanhedrin …"; and of course, we remember that the Sanhedrin dictated all calendar matters.

This is commonly understood then to mean that we are to follow the instructions of the Hillel calendar, as those who composed it had the authority of Moses. It is taught that they even had <u>authority over Scripture,</u> and the people are to obey their Rabbinical mandates, even if they are wrong. If that is so, we should follow the calendar they set forth without question or exception, even if it directly contradicts Scripture. An example might be: The Hillel calendar of today's priesthood tells us to observe Pentecost on Sivan 6 each year, which would be on Sunday only about 1/7 of the time. Leviticus 23:15-16, however, clearly shows us that Pentecost should always be on Sunday. To truly abide by the instructions of today's priesthood, we should honor their Hillel calendar, and would be obliged to honor Pentecost on Sivan 6 in spite of the clearly written Torah instruction by Yahweh to Moses stating the contrary.

However, how can this practice be true and this understanding of Matthew 23:2-3 be valid if even Y'shua Himself refused to subscribe to the instructions of the Pharisees of His day? Matthew also relates that side of the equation:

Matthew 15:1-6
(1) Then came to Jesus scribes and Pharisees, which were of Jerusalem, saying,
(2) Why do thy disciples transgress the tradition of the elders? for they wash not their hands when they eat bread.
(3) But he answered and said unto them, Why do ye also transgress the commandment of God by your tradition?

(4) For God commanded, saying, Honour thy father and mother: and, He that curseth father or mother, let him die the death.

(5) But ye say, Whosoever shall say to his father or his mother, It is a gift, by whatsoever thou mightest be profited by me;

(6) And honour not his father or his mother, he shall be free. Thus have ye made the commandment of God of none effect by your tradition.

Would Y'shua dictate that we are to do what He would not do? Furthermore, if indeed the Zadokite calendar was the one being used by Y'shua when He was here, then He obviously followed the lead of the Zadokite priesthood by discounting the calendar ordained by the ruling priesthood of His day. If it was not wrong for Him to do so, then why should it be wrong for us to do so?

We realize that Y'shua taught in the synagogues, and it is reasonable to question why He did not try to correct the calendar at that time. We have no way of knowing that He did not try. We do know that they did not always like what He tried to tell them, and they sought repeatedly to kill him. We simply rest in the fact that in His time here, He chose to disregard their instruction at times, and for that He must have had good reason.

The Karaite Jews are very committed to righteous living, and even they do not follow the instructions provided by the Hillel calendar, but (as shown above), they keep their own calendar instead.

Nehemia Gordon is a Biblical scholar. He is a Karaite Jew with a background in academia, with a Master's degree in Biblical Studies and a Bachelor's degree in Archaeology from the Hebrew University of Jerusalem, as well as considerable experience in translating the Hebrew text. In order to get to the bottom of the matter, he searched through ancient manuscripts that had been tucked away in the archives of Jewish scribes. The information he shares in his teachings and has recorded in his book The Hebrew Yeshua vs. the Greek Jesus is rather revealing. He indicates that the British Library manuscript of Shem Tov's Hebrew Matthew harbors the answer. His teaching on the subject is readily available for your reference on Youtube as well as in his book. He provides the English translation of the actual Hebrew manuscript for the troubling Matthew passage above. It is:

https://www.youtube.com/watch?v=tddCNY6U77Y -
Matthew 23:2-3
*The Pharisees and sages sit upon the seat of Moses. Therefore all that **he** says to you, diligently do, but according to their reforms (takanot) and their precedents (ma'asim) do not do, because they talk but they do not so.*

The primary difference is simply a plural form (they) in the Greek vs. a singular form (he) in the Hebrew. The word "they" in the Greek implies a reference back to the Pharisees and the scribes (sages), whereas the word "he" in the Hebrew refers back to Moses himself. This one critical element makes all of the difference in the world, and it validates the actions and words of Y'shua as He relates to the Pharisees later in Matthew chapter 15. Identifying this discrepancy is critical to our understanding, as it clarifies that it is Moses (and his **written** Torah instructions) that we are to abide by. It not only frees us from having to adhere to the ways of "the scribes and the Pharisees", but we are actually cautioned to refrain from their ways. The Hebrew version of Matthew actually brings into question the **oral** Torah teachings they embrace and propagate: "but according to their reforms and their precedents do not do, because they talk but they do not so". Maybe these reforms and precedents is somewhat associated with the leaven of the Pharisees and the Sadducees that Y'shua warned us about.

Nehemia Gordon also relates that the Pharisees believe not in one Torah, but in two. They revere what they call the "oral Torah" with the same veneration that they view the written Torah. Though the "oral Torah" teachings are believed to have been given in the days of Moses, these teachings were passed down verbally through many generations before they were finally committed to paper about 200 to 900 AD. They are comprised of the Mishna (200 AD), the Jerusalem Talmud (350 AD), the Babylonian Talmud (500 AD), and the Midrash (200 – 900 AD).

Oracles and the Oral Torah

Referring to Paul's letter to the Romans for a moment, we see a reference to the oracles of God, and find that they were given to the Jews. Before we go to the actual verse, let us clarify who the "Jews" of this passage might be. The term "Jews" in the following passage is Strong's G2453 (Ioudaios). Though his spelling is a slight variation, Spiros Zodhiates, Th.D defines this same Greek word by saying:

The Complete Word Study Dictionary New Testament – General Editor, Spiros Zodhiates, Th.D. – p. 779 - *...after the division of the ten tribes, Ioudaioi, Jews, signified subjects of the kingdom of Judah ... . After the Babylonian captivity, the name "Jews" was extended to all the descendants of Israel who retained the Jewish religion, whether they belonged to the two or the ten tribes and whether or not they returned to Judah ... . It is in this extensive sense that the word is applied in the NT ... .*

Therefore, we see that the Jews designated in Romans would have related to all who were observing the Jewish religion, and not exclusively to the descendants of the tribe of Judah as some suppose. Proceeding on to the Scriptural reference of Romans, we see that to these "Jews" was committed the oracles of Yahweh:

Romans 3:1-2
(1) What advantage then hath the Jew? or what profit is there of circumcision?
(2) Much every way: chiefly, because that <u>unto them were committed the oracles of God</u>.

There are three other New Testament references to this word "oracles", and all are the same Greek word – Strong's G3051 (logion) – *a **divine oracle**, **the words or utterances of God**, **the context of the Mosaic law***. Some say these oracles included the oral Torah. We see from its definition that the oracles would be the divine words of Yahweh, as in the words of the "written Torah" which Moses faithfully recorded immediately. Though they might also have included a broader application known as the "oral Torah", it would surely be limited to the actual divine utterances of Yahweh Himself. However, these actual divine utterances of Yahweh Himself which would have been delivered in the days of Moses may not be at all the same words that have been recorded as the supposed oral Torah used today (the Talmud, Midrash, and Mishna). We simply do not believe these recordings to be the actual direct utterances of Yahweh. As referenced above, the "oral law" was not recorded for many years, and it may have been augmented from one generation to another by the one teaching it. Throughout the generations each orator may have offered some of his own interpretation, spawning one individual spin after another as the years passed by. What was eventually then recorded would likely have been far removed from that which was originally received as Yahweh's divine utterance. Such a conjecture can easily be realized when reading the multitude of views expressed in midrashic writings.

Though the original intent of the oral Torah appears to have been to clarify the written Torah instructions, it appears that over the years the waters may have been muddied considerably by diverse human interpretation. It now has more the flavor of a commentary than direct instruction of Yahweh, and the commentators are often even in disagreement with one another. While we acknowledge that more than one interpretation can be correct, and that a person can certainly glean some wonderful feedback from this work, we feel that the validity of the original oral Word given by Yahweh has been considerably compromised over time and that today's oral Torah can surely no longer be viewed as divine or as an authoritative reference.

The teachings of this oral Torah at the time of Y'shua might actually have been the source of the traditions of men that Y'shua criticized in Matthew 15:6 above when he said they had "made the commandment of God of none effect". Some believe because the Jews were given the oral Torah, that nothing they say or do can be fallible. That would include the part they played in developing the Hillel calendar. For the reasons we have shown, we cannot subscribe to their infallibility in any respect, and do not see that Yahweh's possible utterance of the oral Torah to this people in days gone by validates in any way the authority of any of today's Rabbinical line on calendar matters. This is especially of concern when we are finding that the dates being declared as Yahweh's holy days on this calendar are almost certainly errant and problematic.

Though it is truly not our purpose to condemn today's priesthood, which has such good intent and has accomplished much for the people of the land, there may be yet another problem. We see that Biblically, Father's true and "everlasting priesthood" must come through the Levitical line of Phinehas, and ultimately then through Zadok. However, the lineage of that priesthood was usurped by the Hasmonean line, so it is even possible that the ruling priesthood from that time forward could be viewed as somewhat spurious. Perhaps the legal title to God's ordained priesthood is actually still maintained within a lineage that remains removed from the local rabbinical authority of our day. Apparently the Zadokite line (descendants of Levi) will take authority yet again during the Millennial Kingdom as a reward for their faithfulness, when even the other "Levites" went astray:

Ezekiel 48:10-11
(10) … and the sanctuary of the LORD shall be in the midst thereof.
(11) It shall be for the priests that are **sanctified of the sons of Zadok**; which have kept my charge, which went not astray when the children of Israel went astray, as the Levites went astray.

Though people today often think of the Zadokite line as being extinct, this simply cannot be. Otherwise, we need to cut the words of Ezekiel from our Bibles. If Yahweh spoke these words through Ezekiel, then the lineage has remained intact, and it WILL reemerge.

The assurance is that the Zadokite lineage will serve during the Millennial reign. The verification regarding the straying of Israel is actually mentioned twice in Ezekiel, the other time being in Ezekiel 44:15. It appears it is worthy of repeat mention! We see by this that both the Levites (apparently, the balance of the priesthood as differentiated from those of the Zadokite line) and the children of Israel (the people) went astray. Only those priests who were of the Zadokite lineage remained faithful. As a result, they will be assisting in the Millennial Temple, yet future. Is it possible that they maintained the truth of the oracles when others started intertwining them with heathen ways? Could the calendar issue have been at the heart of this matter? The type of straying meant here is not totally understood, but the scrolls which speak of the sons of Zadok do seem to concur that the departure of the Zadokite priests from the Temple was because of something being done by some acting priests of that day which the Zadokites believed had defiled the Temple. Those of the Zadokite lineage could not abide by or participate in such errant practice, and either left through disdain or were forced out from the Temple grounds because they would not condone such practice.

Quoting again from Davies, Brooke, and Callaway, we see confirmation of this potential:

<u>The Complete World of the Dead Sea Scrolls</u> - by Philip R. Davies, George J. Brooke, & Phillip R. Callaway
- p. 46 -

But since the Temple Scroll (p. 156), for example, describes a different liturgical cycle, and many of the scrolls a different calendar, from that known from other sources, it may be that either different groups shared the Temple, each observing its own rules, or the regime changed as different groups were accorded control of it. Certainly, it is difficult to explain otherwise how deviant Temple calendars and regimes could have developed. The imposition of a single Temple regime and calendar, and the prohibition of access to those following any other system, may help to explain why at least one group reflected in the scrolls felt it necessary to secede from Temple worship and form themselves into a sect.

Since there is evidence that the calendar in use by some of the Temple priests who had taken charge was different, and the words in some scrolls condemn that calendar so thoroughly, it is entirely possible that this was the basic source of contention. It seems the writers of <u>The Book of Jubilees</u> viewed the observance of Yahweh's feast days on the wrong dates as a very grievous error which mixed the clean with the unclean and the holy with the unholy. This then may well have been the only reason necessary for their departure, as we are finding no other indicators of disagreement between them.

CHAPTER 19

CONSIDERATIONS ABOUT THIS WORK

Let's switch gears for a moment and relate all of this to today's reality. How does it all fit in the lives of each of us as Believers? As we approached some whom we greatly respect in the Hebraic Roots movement to mention our research, we were asked some questions, cautioned to be certain about our findings, and advised to be careful about the timing for releasing our findings. The considerations we have pondered during the remainder of this process are listed below.

Why Would God Choose Us to Reveal This?

It is a fair question – one which we ourselves have repeatedly pondered.

Actually, our voices are not alone in this proclamation. It was through ideas expressed by others that our interest was spurred to pursue the truth regarding this potential.

Perhaps Father chose us to join in this venture simply because we were willing vessels. We are not theologically trained and heavily invested in a vast ministry that teaches the more standard calendar. Therefore, changing course was not as difficult for us as it would be for some. We were somewhat invested, having been dedicated to the study of the soli-lunar calendar for some time. We had actually even produced our own printed calendars relative to the lunar cycle on a small scale for friends. Our time and monetary investment in this venture was quite insignificant though, when compared to others.

When the potential of a "non" lunar calendar first came to light, we wanted to reject it outright, but something within would not allow for that. Feeling prompted by the Spirit, we were willing to devote the time to pursue lengthy research and record our findings. Actually, we were hoping to disprove it promptly and put it behind us, but that was not to be. We continually bathed the entire process in a GREAT DEAL of prayer that the Holy Spirit would guide our research efforts and lead us to Father's total Truth:

John 16:13
(13) Howbeit when he, the Spirit of truth, is come, he will <u>guide you into all truth</u>: for he shall not speak of himself; but whatsoever he shall hear, that shall he speak: and he will shew you things to come.

We felt that we should be able to rest in this, due to Y'shua's words in Matthew:

Matthew 7:7-11
(7) <u>Ask, and it shall be given you; seek, and ye shall find; knock, and it shall be opened unto you</u>:
(8) For every one that asketh receiveth; and he that seeketh findeth; and to him that knocketh it shall be opened.
(9) Or what man is there of you, whom if his son ask bread, will he give him a stone?

(10) Or if he ask a fish, will he give him a serpent?
(11) If ye then, being evil, know how to give good gifts unto your children, how much more shall your Father which is in heaven give good things to them that ask him?

Even with the understanding that we would be led to Father's Truth, it was still an absolutely amazing journey to uncover verifications, one after another, that the theory we were trying to disprove was actually being proven before our eyes.

A passage in 1 Corinthians may be somewhat relevant here:

1 Corinthians 1:26-31
(26) For ye see your calling, brethren, how that not many wise men after the flesh, not many mighty, not many noble, are called:
(27) But God hath chosen the foolish things of the world to confound the wise; and God hath chosen the weak things of the world to confound the things which are mighty;
(28) And base things of the world, and things which are despised, hath God chosen, yea, and things which are not, to bring to nought things that are:
(29) That no flesh should glory in his presence.
(30) But of him are ye in Christ Jesus, who of God is made unto us wisdom, and righteousness, and sanctification, and redemption:
(31) That, according as it is written, He that glorieth, let him glory in the Lord.

In this instance, that seems to fit like a glove. Maybe "weak things" (some nobodies like us) could actually be used as the chosen means to open eyes and confound the "things which are mighty" (the established system used by one of the greatest of religious institutions today – established Rabbinic authority). While we realize that it sounds ludicrous, it is a Biblically sound principle that was recorded in our Bibles for a purpose. It may just be Father's way!

It is not exactly with trepidation that we expose our findings now to public scrutiny, because we are not to be in fear when walking in the Spirit. However, it does cause us a significant degree of sorrow to confront what has been such a part of our lives and the lives of others. The lunar method had been very near and dear to us. However, now that we are seeing it through Father's eyes, we have had to deal with it before Him and move on into the knowledge He has revealed to us. We are retracting our previous stance and moving into the light He has shown us. It puts us in an awkward place relative to the brethren we love, but is anything Father asks of us too much to bear? We think not. We will work through that with Him one day at a time as we choose to observe His holy days according to the Zadokite calendar and share our findings with others.

CHAPTER 20

DOES IT REALLY MATTER?

Finally, we had to look at whether the publication of this book would be worth all of the upheaval it might potentially cause within the Hebraic Roots movement we hold so dear. We came face to face with that answer very recently.

Stones – Are We Gathering, or Scattering?

Apparently, it was not just the Zadokite lineage that viewed the Temple practice to be problematic. Y'shua prophesied that the Temple of His day would be dismantled, leaving not one stone on another. Indeed, history verifies that in 70 AD, shortly after the His resurrection, this is precisely what happened. Through divine judgment, the Temple was destroyed, scattering the stones that had formed its structure.

The words of Y'shua as recorded in Luke may be very meaningful:

Luke 11:23
(23) He that is not with me is against me: and he that gathereth not with me scattereth.

Maybe we have an obligation to help Y'shua gather the stones back together to rebuild in truth that which was scattered due to error. His Millennial Temple must ultimately be built, and probably in pretty short order. If we are not helping Him put the truth back into place for the building of this Temple, then He indicates that we may be seen as continuing the scattering process and working against Him. Once we know the truth, we are not to walk the fence. If we are not helping, we are hindering.

According to Peter, we are to be "lively stones", building up a spiritual house.

1 Peter 2:5
(5) Ye also, as lively stones, are built up a spiritual house, an holy priesthood, to offer up spiritual sacrifices, acceptable to God by Jesus Christ.

We do not want this spiritual house (Temple) to be considered defiled by participating in some type of errant practice. Just as the defiled physical Temple structure was destroyed through judgment, so our spiritual Temple may face consequences:

1 Corinthians 3:17
(17) If any man defile the temple of God, him shall God destroy; for the temple of God is holy, which temple ye are.

We do not mean to imply that Father is ready to destroy us immediately if we have been observing the wrong calendar! However, it does mean that He does not want us to continue in error once truth has been presented. That is the thought being cited in Acts:

Acts 17:30
(30) And the times of this ignorance God winked at; but now commandeth all men every where to repent:

We are held accountable when we have been confronted with truth. What will we do with it?

The Pope and the Priesthood

It is by a somewhat nebulous Scriptural text that the Catholics believe that Peter was the "stone" upon which the church was built. Accordingly, they view the present Pope as having the authority to dictate the change of Father's weekly holy Sabbath from the 7th day to the 1st, even though that mandate totally contradicts the words Father gave Moses. Does that belief make it right to observe Sabbath on Sunday? Should we go back to Sunday worship to align to the supposed "Scripturally derived" authority of the Pope to change Father's appointed times as he sees fit? Though there may be a literal Antichrist figure, the spirit of Antichrist has been active for many years! We see in Daniel that one of the prophesied accomplishments might already have been accomplished:

Daniel 7:25
(25) And he shall speak great words against the most High, and shall wear out the saints of the most High, and think to change times and laws: and they shall be given into his hand until a time and times and the dividing of time.

Could the Christian version have been distorted to "change times" relative to His WEEKLY Sabbaths, and the Hebraic version have been likewise distorted to "change times" relative to Father's ANNUAL Sabbaths? Are we not dealing with the same type of thing here? It seems that the Scriptural authority of the **priesthood** to impose their choice for Yahweh's **annual** Sabbath days is very closely akin to the Scriptural authority of the **Pope** to impose his choice for Yahweh's **weekly** Sabbath days. Maybe there is leaven in both the Christian and the Jewish loaves. One more time we will mention Y'shua's warning of the leaven in the instruction of the Pharisees and the Sadducees:

Matthew 16:11-12
(11) How is it that ye do not understand that I spake it not to you concerning bread, that ye should beware of the leaven of the Pharisees and of the Sadducees?
(12) Then understood they how that he bade them not beware of the leaven of bread, but of the doctrine of the Pharisees and of the Sadducees.

The word "doctrine" here is Strong's G1322 (didachē) – *teaching, that which is taught, instruction.*

If we don't revere the Pope's instruction regarding Yahweh's weekly Sabbath observation because we view it as leaven, then we might want to look at how we view the priesthood's instruction regarding Yahweh's annual Sabbath observations, (as well as their method of determining these days), which could be leaven as well. The discovery of Hebraic Roots by Christendom has begun our restoration back into the correct timing for WEEKLY Sabbath observance – regardless of the Papal mandates to the contrary. Maybe it is now time for Father's Truth in ANNUAL Sabbath timing to come back into prominence, regardless of the modern Judaic mandates to the contrary. If indeed the lunar calendric system was derived from the Babylonians as a result of Israel's captivity, then its roots are steeped in heathen adulterous ideology which Yahweh repeatedly and soundly condemned.

Note here that the enemy's time is limited. There will be an end to this travesty. Is that end now approaching? Is it the destiny of our day to begin transition back to Father's Truth?

Combining Two Sticks

There is a school of thought that indicates that Christians today (typological of the house of Ephraim) are often missing the understanding of Torah as the roots of their faith. On the other side of the spectrum, those of the Jewish faith (typological of the house of Judah) are missing the understanding that Y'shua is the Messiah, the savior for mankind. Each group has need of what the other has to offer. We concur adamantly. These two groups must come together. Yahweh prophesied that they would, and His prophecy is certain to come to pass:

Ezekiel 37:16-17
(16) Moreover, thou son of man, take thee one stick, and write upon it, For <u>Judah,</u> and for the children of Israel his companions: then take another stick, and write upon it, For Joseph, the stick of <u>Ephraim,</u> and for all the house of Israel his companions:
(17) And <u>join them one to another into one stick; and they shall become one in thine hand.</u>

In fact, this process seems to have begun, and is now underway. Christians are finding their Hebraic roots, and those of the Jewish faith are coming to understand their Messiah. The consensus is that as Believers embrace the Torah and its ways, it assists in the uniting of the two sticks. It is also thought that Believers keeping the Hillel calendar is a major part of this impetus. There is concern that this progress will come to a halt if the calendar of the current priesthood is brought into question. In other words, the unity which is beginning to come about may be jeopardized if the new calendar surfaces. However, we must ask: "Is a unity built upon falsehood acceptable to Father?" "Is it the way He intends His unity to come about, or should the unity which evolves be built upon His Truth and equipped to draw His children from both sides together around that Truth?" If the Hillel calendar is used in the formation of this union, then perhaps it would be built under a banner of error. Conversely, if validity of the proper calendar was revealed, accepted, and adopted universally, the union could be formed under the banner of truth. Any setback in progress would be temporal, and the end result would actually serve to strengthen the unity! It may actually be a step toward the restoration of the prophesied Zadokite priesthood in the Millennial Kingdom setting.

The surfacing of these scrolls at just such a time as this might well have been ordained in order to set things right again <u>in preparation for</u> the Millennial Temple which should soon be built. Since the Zadokites went underground, it is thought that the ability to track their bloodline has been lost. However, as we mentioned before, it cannot have become extinct, or Ezekiel's twice-spoken words of prophecy would have to be rendered fallible and untrustworthy. The blood-line must have continued, though those who have any remnant of this blood are presently unknown to us. It is very interesting that there have been recent reports of an effort to use DNA matches to locate this bloodline. Perhaps those who will ultimately pick up the reigns to restore the correct calendar version on a priestly level will be those who bare a bit of the bloodline from that lineage. It may well be time for that portion of the transition to occur.

CHAPTER 21

TYING IT ALL TOGETHER

The lunar method of determining the timing for our months and years simply does not relate conclusively to our agricultural productivity. The festivals, in turn, are in direct correlation with our agriculture, and must be timed appropriately to correspond with the harvesting of our crops. The heat and light of the sun are the essential ingredients to produce the growth of our crops. When the timing of our months is in conjunction with the solar guidelines Father placed in the heavens, the spring equinox (dictated by the sun) will signal the proper time to begin our year. The months will then unfold in simplistic fashion, by His precise patterning. The patterning of His sevens and twelves will bring rotation to the calendar as the weeks and months are completed, and the festivals will occur on the proper days within that simple monthly schedule. God IS NOT the author of confusion. The calendar we now see as being His true calendar is remarkably simplistic and accurate, bringing in the festivals at just the right time in each yearly cycle. The harvests will always be ready when they arrive. The festivals will never be too early or too late to match the harvest seasons - which are dependent on God's proportionate amounts of heat and light from the sun. There is never a question of when the new month or year will begin. Not only can it be determined in advance, but it will be perfect in its unfolding year after year.

Yom Kippur will never occur on Sabbath, and all of the other festival dates will be on appropriate days as well. Each feast day will always occur on the same day of the week, year after year. Feast of Trumpets and Tabernacles will always begin on weekday 4, Passover will always be on weekday 3, etc. The confusion and uncertainty, as well as the problems associated with postponements on the Hillel calendar will be a thing of the past. Isn't that what Father would intend? Because He Himself is not a God of confusion, neither would He want us to be in a continual state of confusion over how to determine His holy days.

The unhappiness of Father with the manner of observance of His holy days will be put in the past as well. If we go back to meeting with Him on the days He specified in the manner He intended, our feast days will no longer be an affront to Him.

Even Mark 14:12-18 points to the change that had taken place with the calendar, as it is impossible to reasonably reconcile Y'shua's Passover dinner with His disciples on the day most theologians want to believe it was. Pastors and teachers have twisted the words of Mark all out of proportion in order to try to make sense of this passage, when the actual reality seems very simple. Y'shua was observing the feast days one day earlier than Temple had ordained them to be observed. The calendar established by the priesthood in Y'shua's day had already been corrupted, and Y'shua was honoring His Father's feast days on the days Father had intended.

Even the waving of the sheaf on day 26 of month 1 (instead of the morrow after the Sabbath associated with the week of Unleavened Bread) makes a great deal of sense when Leviticus 23:5-14, Exodus 29:29-35, and Numbers 19:11-19 are studied with new eyes. It is then possible to see that this supposed anomaly in the calendar really has a place in Scripture. There seems to be a distinct close of one thought and beginning of another between verse 8 and verse 9 of Leviticus 23. Verse 8 <u>concludes</u> the section of Unleavened Bread. Then verse 9 starts a new thought when Yahweh addresses Moses a second time. If it had been intended to be conjoined to that week, there would have been no need for the <u>separation</u> of instruction by Yahweh to Moses that starts with verse 9. Verse 9 is short and simply starts another segment by saying, "And Yahweh spake unto Moses saying". Verse 10 then begins His instructions for the wave offering. The only time frame given was that it was to be on the morrow after the sabbath (verse 11) when they entered the land <u>and reaped the harvest</u> (verse 10). The timing for this waving is clearly linked here to the reaping of their harvest rather than to the week of Unleavened Bread.

It seems to us that if the waving was to take place DURING the week of Unleavened Bread, there would have been significantly more intricate instructions within the verses 1-8 section to explain precisely how it related to that week. On the present calendar, that week begins on different weekdays on different years. There is a great deal of confusion as to when the waving should occur. The presumption that the waving is linked to the week of Unleavened Bread has led to at least three different versions for the timing of wave offering, dependent upon which Jewish or Messianic sect you are working with. Maybe the lack of clarity in determining the proper timing for the week is because it should not be interpreted as being in conjunction with that week at all!

It took a while for what we had once been taught to be put behind us, but now it really does make sense to us that the performing of the wave offering in conjunction with the week of Unleavened Bread may merely be a long-held tradition that began with the departure from the former calendar. It fits well with the view of the Friday to Sunday theory from crucifixion to resurrection that is taught in Christendom as well. We DO wish there was more that had been recorded to explain why the time-line was configured as it was in the Dead Sea Scrolls records, but we do see that its calendar instructions are actually a better fit with what Scripture literally says. In reality, having searched Leviticus 23 with honest intent, we now see no Scriptural conflict with the 26th day of month 1 at all.

Secondly, when we look at all of the ceremonial aspects of Father's ways, it does ring true that Y'shua would have to have been cleansed from the impurity of His death experience for a week after His resurrection, in accordance with Torah instructions. Please note that this would have ABSOLUTELY nothing to do with His "spiritual" state of holiness, but it would relate only to the defilement that naturally occurs through the death process. Death is equated with an unclean state - a major matter of concern in Torah. When people touch something unclean, they are normally unclean just until even. Touching a dead body, however, is more serious, and the cleansing is more involved. Torah says that the one who touches a dead body is "unclean" until after the seventh day - period. Their spiritual state or standing is simply irrelevant. Torah was patterned after the heavenly design, so there is really no reason to presume that such ceremonial observance would be waived in the heavenly rendering.

Likewise, Torah instructions indicate that a priest must be consecrated for a week before being able to assume His role as priest. Again, the spiritual condition of the priest being consecrated was irrelevant. Since the earthly instructions were based on heavenly patterns, it seems obvious that these same patterns would be enacted in the heavenly realm as well. The Bible tells us that Y'shua's crucifixion and resurrection were ordained from the beginning of the world. Might not this pattern have been established in order for the transition of the earthly Y'shua to the heavenly role of our High Priest that He would enter into after His resurrection? Only Father knows what the ceremonial laws of Heaven dictate. There would obviously be some, as the Word hints of a heavenly priesthood through the words that relate to Melchizedek. After the completion of Y'ahua's purification and consecration, He would be CEREMONIALLY ready to be waved as the First Fruits of the dead, and/or to wave those who arose after His resurrection as His First Fruits offering as well, fulfilling Hebrews 8:3.

While the timing of the Passover and the waving of the sheaf were initially troublesome to us, they ended up pointing conclusively to the validity of the Zadokite calendar, and the corruption of the calendar currently observed by the priesthood. Understanding all of these things from a new perspective points more than ever to the distortions which may have evolved when the former calendar was changed to what we have today. While we are certainly NOT trying to place blame for the manner in which such corruption may have occurred, we are trying to relay evidence that it may be incorrect, and to put emphasis on the validity we are finding. Neither are we insensitive to the hearts of the people today who continue to use the calendar we believe was corrupted. We observed it too until we studied it out more completely. We are simply praying that the understanding we have come to embrace might become real to you as well. It might be very important that others begin to see this in the days ahead! Conclusively, we believe that a strong consideration of the Zadokite calendar is warranted!

There seems to be is a total lack of evidence that anything resembling our current lunar-based calendar was being used in the days of Moses. Actually, there is a great deal of implication that Moses and Hebrew people under His charge were using the calendar that is now coming to light. How then do we reconcile the transition away from what Father would have shown Moses to what we now observe? Why are our Bibles strangely silent relative to the mention of (or even the description of) a crescent moon or the physical act of sighting it? Where is the reference to months of different lengths, or years with an extra month? While the Biblical calendar may still be a somewhat cloudy picture, we feel that the study we have worked through has shed a beam of light on the subject that had been missing over the years. It is, in fact, enough light to be able to form a sketchy version of the calendar we are now personally using. We feel it has brought us one step closer to spending intimate time with Abba our Father on the exact days He asked us to meet with Him.

What actually is our personal obligation in choosing when to observe of Father's festivals? Wouldn't he desire that we observe them correctly? If we see that those who are dictating the dates are using invalid criteria for their selection, what is our part in helping them to recognize the deviations and change course? Might the end result be the ability to keep a simplistic and comprehensive calendar on a corporate basis that will please Father? How might we be misunderstanding our Biblical ques regarding calendar determination? Incorrect calendar references may actually have led us to celebrate with all types of feasting and festivities for day 1 of Succoth on what is actually Yom Kippur, the most somber day of the year when Father specified that we are to afflict our souls.

We certainly don't want to profane the Father by mixing His clean with the unclean, and by mixing His specific sanctioned holy days with ones which are common. If the Creator of the universe has scheduled appointed days for His creation to meet with Him, should not his creation care enough to be sure they keep their appointments with Him on the days He specified? That only happens if the right calendar is being used. We have come to view unity (even of the Hebrew Roots community) around an errant calendar as unsuitable. It would be unity of a sort, but at what cost? What and where is the truth in this whole issue? That is for each of us to decide, and it may be an important decision! Selah (ponder these things)! May we do so prayerfully.

EPILOGUE

Please scrutinize what we have drawn together, and prayerfully consider what this information holds for you individually. Also, please feel free to correspond. Any considerately worded thoughts and comments are welcome.

Correspondence pro or con, as well as requests for information regarding calendars, digital or hardcopy tremplates, or more books can be sent to:

Bill and Karen Bishop
P. O. Box 64
Glasgow, KY 42142

or -- you can e-mail us at:
2trees@disciples.com

or -- you can contact us through our website:
returningtothegarden.com

INTRODUCTION TO APPENDICES – MAKING YOUR OWN CALENDAR

The appendices that follow will enable you to keep the calendar throughout the future. You will find extensive templates, data, and schemata that provide a means of determining and charting the calendar year on blank copies for your own personal use. We believe we have included absolutely everything you will need to accommodate this calendar system through the year 2100. If you find that using the book to reproduce the templates is difficult, please let us know using the contact information in the Epilogue, and we will provide a digital or hardcopy version by mail to make your reproduction easier.

You may find, however, a more pleasing option in obtaining one of our informative, professionally printed calendars. They are a spiral-bound, hanging type of monthly calendar, based on the Biblical months. The primary basis of our printed calendars is the Zadokite formula outlined in this book. They begin in the spring with Month I – Day 1, and go through the 12 months. The corresponding Hillel and Gregorian dates are shown with each Zadokite date to easily facilitate cross-referencing to the other major calendars. All significant religious and secular holidays are noted for each calendar system, as well as new and full moons, solstices, and equinoxes, according to sunset times in Jerusalem. Sabbaths, high holy days, and feasts are clearly marked.

Instead of using pictures above the fold, we provide a listing of historical events from the Bible for each month. Along with the events are the dates they occurred and their corresponding verse references. In the past, many people have favorably remarked about how much they enjoy having this information readily available on the calendar.

We offer these calendars at cost plus shipping which is currently around $14-$16 total. Hopefully by the time you are reading this, our cost per calendar will have become lower, due to a greater volume of demand. One main objective is to simply share this calendar at the lowest possible cost with anyone who is interested. Please contact us using the contact information in the Epilogue.

Appendix 1 – Major Events on Zadokite Calendar

The following chart lists the major events that occur during the Zadokite calendar year. It shows the date of the year these events fall each and every year, as well as the progressive day of the year that they occur.

Please note that the festival of Purim occurs between January 1 (the start of the Gregorian calendar) and the Vernal equinox. Since this appendix is designed to flow with the Gregorian calendar, Purim is put at the beginning of the year, even though it ends the previous Zadokite year.

Special Event	Hebrew Date	Progressive Date
Purim	XII – 14	347
Shushan Purim	XII – 15	348
Chodesh (Spring)	XII – 31	364
New Year (Beginning of Months)	I – 1	1
Passover	I – 14	14
Feast of Unleavened Bread – Day 1	I – 15	15
Feast of Unleavened Bread – Day 7	I – 21	21
Waiving of the First Fruit (Barley)	I – 26	26
Pentecost	III – 15	75
Chodesh (Summer)	III – 31	91
Chodesh (Fall)	VI – 31	182
Feast of Trumpets	VII – 1	183
Day of Atonement	VII – 10	192
Feast of Tabernacles – Day 1	VII – 15	197
Feast of Tabernacles – Day 8	VII – 22	204
Chanukkah – Day 1	IX – 25	267
Chodesh (Winter)	IX – 31	273
Chanukkah – Day 8	X – 1	274

Appendix 2 – Schema for Typical Zadokite Calendar Year
The schema in this appendix provides a template for the typical Zadokite calendar year. Each progressive 3-month period repeats the pattern. Months I, IV, VII, and X are alike, months II, V, VIII, and XI are alike, and months III, VI, IX, and XII are alike. The single exception is when an extra week is needed, and put at the end of month XII. Please turn to the next page for the schema.

Schema for Typical Zadokite Calendar Year

I

1	2	3	4	5	6	7
			1	2	3	4
5	6	7	8	9	10	11
12	13	14	15	16	17	18
19	20	21	22	23	24	25
26	27	28	29	30		

II

1	2	3	4	5	6	7
					1	2
3	4	5	6	7	8	9
10	11	12	13	14	15	16
17	18	19	20	21	22	23
24	25	26	27	28	29	30

III

1	2	3	4	5	6	7
1	2	3	4	5	6	7
8	9	10	11	12	13	14
15	16	17	18	19	20	21
22	23	24	25	26	27	28
29	30	31				

IV

1	2	3	4	5	6	7
			1	2	3	4
5	6	7	8	9	10	11
12	13	14	15	16	17	18
19	20	21	22	23	24	25
26	27	28	29	30		

V

1	2	3	4	5	6	7
					1	2
3	4	5	6	7	8	9
10	11	12	13	14	15	16
17	18	19	20	21	22	23
24	25	26	27	28	29	30

VI

1	2	3	4	5	6	7
1	2	3	4	5	6	7
8	9	10	11	12	13	14
15	16	17	18	19	20	21
22	23	24	25	26	27	28
29	30	31				

VII

1	2	3	4	5	6	7
			1	2	3	4
5	6	7	8	9	10	11
12	13	14	15	16	17	18
19	20	21	22	23	24	25
26	27	28	29	30		

VIII

1	2	3	4	5	6	7
					1	2
3	4	5	6	7	8	9
10	11	12	13	14	15	16
17	18	19	20	21	22	23
24	25	26	27	28	29	30

IX

1	2	3	4	5	6	7
1	2	3	4	5	6	7
8	9	10	11	12	13	14
15	16	17	18	19	20	21
22	23	24	25	26	27	28
29	30	31				

X

1	2	3	4	5	6	7
			1	2	3	4
5	6	7	8	9	10	11
12	13	14	15	16	17	18
19	20	21	22	23	24	25
26	27	28	29	30		

XI

1	2	3	4	5	6	7
					1	2
3	4	5	6	7	8	9
10	11	12	13	14	15	16
17	18	19	20	21	22	23
24	25	26	27	28	29	30

XII

1	2	3	4	5	6	7
1	2	3	4	5	6	7
8	9	10	11	12	13	14
15	16	17	18	19	20	21
22	23	24	25	26	27	28
29	30	31				

Appendix 3 – Gregorian Dates for Zadokite Events Through 2100

Using a few charts and tables has enabled us to provide the following information for the reader. The data for Gregorian dates that correspond to Zadokite events is posted here for the years 2017 through 2100

Special Event	Week Day	Zadokite Date	Gregorian 2011	Gregorian 2012	Gregorian 2013	Gregorian 2014	Gregorian 2015	Gregorian 2016	Gregorian 2017	Gregorian 2018	Gregorian 2019	Gregorian 2020
Purim	Sa	XII - 14							3/4	3/3	3/2	3/7
Shushan Purim	Su	XII - 15							3/5	3/4	3/3	3/8
Chodesh – Spring	Tu	XII - 31							3/21	3/20	3/19	3/24
New Year	W	I - 1							3/22	3/21	3/27	3/25
Passover	Tu	I - 14							4/4	4/3	4/9	4/7
Unleavened Br - 1	W	I - 15							4/5	4/4	4/10	4/8
Unleavened Br - 7	Tu	I - 21							4/11	4/10	4/16	4/14
Wave 1st Fruits	Su	I - 26							4/16	4/15	4/21	4/19
Pentecost	Su	III - 15							6/4	6/3	6/9	6/7
Chodesh – Summer	Tu	III - 31							6/20	6/19	6/25	6/23
Chodesh - Fall	Tu	VI - 31							9/19	9/18	9/24	9/22
Trumpets	W	VII - 1							9/20	9/19	9/25	9/23
Atonement	F	VII - 10							9/29	9/28	10/4	10/2
Tabernacles - 1	W	VII - 15							10/4	10/3	10/9	10/7
Tabernacles - 8	W	VII - 22							10/11	10/10	10/16	10/14
Chanukkah - 1	W	IX - 25							12/13	12/12	12/18	12/16
Chodesh – Winter	Tu	IX - 31							12/19	12/18	12/24	12/22
Chanukkah - 8	W	X - 1							12/20	12/19	12/25	12/23

102

Appendix 3 – Gregorian Dates for Zadokite Events Through 2100

Special Event	Week Day	Zadokite Date	Gregorian 2021	Gregorian 2022	Gregorian 2023	Gregorian 2024	Gregorian 2025	Gregorian 2026	Gregorian 2027	Gregorian 2028	Gregorian 2029	Gregorian 2030
Purim	Sa	XII - 14	3/6	3/5	3/4	3/2	3/1	3/7	3/6	3/4	3/3	3/2
Shushan Purim	Su	XII - 15	3/7	3/6	3/5	3/3	3/2	3/8	3/7	3/5	3/4	3/3
Chodesh – Spring	Tu	XII - 31	3/23	3/22	3/21	3/19	3/18	3/24	3/23	3/21	3/20	3/19
New Year	W	I - 1	3/24	3/23	3/22	3/20	3/26	3/25	3/24	3/22	3/21	3/20
Passover	Tu	I - 14	4/6	4/5	4/4	4/2	4/8	4/7	4/6	4/4	4/3	4/2
Unleavened Br - 1	W	I - 15	4/7	4/6	4/5	4/3	4/9	4/8	4/7	4/5	4/4	4/3
Unleavened Br - 7	Tu	I - 21	4/13	4/12	4/11	4/9	4/15	4/14	4/13	4/11	4/10	4/9
Wave 1st Fruits	Su	I - 26	4/18	4/17	4/16	4/14	4/20	4/19	4/18	4/16	4/15	4/14
Pentecost	Su	III - 15	6/6	6/5	6/4	6/2	6/8	6/7	6/6	6/4	6/3	6/2
Chodesh – Summer	Tu	III - 31	6/22	6/21	6/20	6/18	6/24	6/23	6/22	6/20	6/19	6/18
Chodesh - Fall	Tu	VI - 31	9/21	9/20	9/19	9/17	9/23	9/22	9/21	9/19	9/18	9/17
Trumpets	W	VII - 1	9/22	9/21	9/20	9/18	9/24	9/23	9/22	9/20	9/19	9/18
Atonement	F	VII - 10	10/1	9/30	9/29	9/27	10/3	10/2	10/1	9/29	9/28	9/27
Tabernacles - 1	W	VII - 15	10/6	10/5	10/4	10/2	10/8	10/7	10/6	10/4	10/3	10/2
Tabernacles - 8	W	VII - 22	10/13	10/12	10/11	10/9	10/15	10/14	10/13	10/11	10/10	10/9
Chanukkah - 1	W	IX - 25	12/15	12/14	12/13	12/11	12/17	12/16	12/15	12/13	12/12	12/11
Chodesh – Winter	Tu	IX - 31	12/21	12/20	12/19	12/17	12/23	12/22	12/21	12/19	12/18	12/17
Chanukkah - 8	W	X - 1	12/22	12/21	12/20	12/18	12/24	12/23	12/22	12/20	12/19	12/18

Appendix 3 – Gregorian Dates for Zadokite Events Through 2100

Special Event	Week Day	Zadokite Date	Gregorian 2031	Gregorian 2032	Gregorian 2033	Gregorian 2034	Gregorian 2035	Gregorian 2036	Gregorian 2037	Gregorian 2038	Gregorian 2039	Gregorian 2040
Purim	Sa	XII - 14	3/1	3/6	3/5	3/4	3/3	3/1	3/7	3/6	3/5	3/3
Shushan Purim	Su	XII - 15	3/2	3/7	3/6	3/5	3/4	3/2	3/8	3/7	3/6	3/4
Chodesh – Spring	Tu	XII - 31	3/18	3/23	3/22	3/21	3/20	3/18	3/24	3/23	3/22	3/20
New Year	W	I - 1	3/26	3/24	3/23	3/22	3/21	3/26	3/25	3/24	3/23	3/21
Passover	Tu	I - 14	4/8	4/6	4/5	4/4	4/3	4/8	4/7	4/6	4/5	4/3
Unleavened Br - 1	W	I - 15	4/9	4/7	4/6	4/5	4/4	4/9	4/8	4/7	4/6	4/4
Unleavened Br - 7	Tu	I - 21	4/15	4/13	4/12	4/11	4/10	4/15	4/14	4/13	4/12	4/10
Wave 1st Fruits	Su	I - 26	4/20	4/18	4/17	4/16	4/15	4/20	4/19	4/18	4/17	4/15
Pentecost	Su	III - 15	6/8	6/6	6/5	6/4	6/3	6/8	6/7	6/6	6/5	6/3
Chodesh – Summer	Tu	III - 31	6/24	6/22	6/21	6/20	6/19	6/24	6/23	6/22	6/21	6/19
Chodesh - Fall	Tu	VI - 31	9/23	9/21	9/20	9/19	9/18	9/23	9/22	9/21	9/20	9/18
Trumpets	W	VII - 1	9/24	9/22	9/21	9/20	9/19	9/24	9/23	9/22	9/21	9/19
Atonement	F	VII - 10	10/3	10/1	9/30	9/29	9/28	10/3	10/2	10/1	9/30	9/28
Tabernacles - 1	W	VII - 15	10/8	10/6	10/5	10/4	10/3	10/8	10/7	10/6	10/5	10/3
Tabernacles - 8	W	VII - 22	10/15	10/13	10/12	10/11	10/10	10/15	10/14	10/13	10/12	10/10
Chanukkah - 1	W	IX - 25	12/17	12/15	12/14	12/13	12/12	12/17	12/16	12/15	12/14	12/12
Chodesh – Winter	Tu	IX - 31	12/23	12/21	12/20	12/19	12/18	12/23	12/22	12/21	12/20	12/18
Chanukkah - 8	W	X - 1	12/24	12/22	12/21	12/20	12/19	12/24	12/23	12/22	12/21	12/19

Appendix 3 – Gregorian Dates for Zadokite Events Through 2100

Special Event	Week Day	Zadokite Date	Gregorian 2041	Gregorian 2042	Gregorian 2043	Gregorian 2044	Gregorian 2045	Gregorian 2046	Gregorian 2047	Gregorian 2048	Gregorian 2049	Gregorian 2050
Purim	Sa	XII - 14	3/2	3/1	3/7	3/5	3/4	3/3	3/2	3/7	3/6	3/5
Shushan Purim	Su	XII - 15	3/3	3/2	3/8	3/6	3/5	3/4	3/3	3/8	3/7	3/6
Chodesh – Spring	Tu	XII - 31	3/19	3/18	3/24	3/22	3/21	3/20	3/19	3/24	3/23	3/22
New Year	W	I - 1	3/20	3/26	3/25	3/23	3/22	3/21	3/27	3/25	3/24	3/23
Passover	Tu	I - 14	4/2	4/8	4/7	4/5	4/4	4/3	4/9	4/7	4/6	4/5
Unleavened Br - 1	W	I - 15	4/3	4/9	4/8	4/6	4/5	4/4	4/10	4/8	4/7	4/6
Unleavened Br - 7	Tu	I - 21	4/9	4/15	4/14	4/12	4/11	4/10	4/16	4/14	4/13	4/12
Wave 1st Fruits	Su	I - 26	4/14	4/20	4/19	4/17	4/16	4/15	4/21	4/19	4/18	4/17
Pentecost	Su	III - 15	6/2	6/8	6/7	6/5	6/4	6/3	6/9	6/7	6/6	6/5
Chodesh – Summer	Tu	III - 31	6/18	6/24	6/23	6/21	6/20	6/19	6/25	6/23	6/22	6/21
Chodesh - Fall	Tu	VI - 31	9/17	9/23	9/22	9/20	9/19	9/18	9/24	9/22	9/21	9/20
Trumpets	W	VII - 1	9/18	9/24	9/23	9/21	9/20	9/19	9/25	9/23	9/22	9/21
Atonement	F	VII - 10	9/27	10/3	10/2	9/30	9/29	9/28	10/4	10/2	10/1	9/30
Tabernacles - 1	W	VII - 15	10/2	10/8	10/7	10/5	10/4	10/3	10/9	10/7	10/6	10/5
Tabernacles - 8	W	VII - 22	10/9	10/15	10/14	10/12	10/11	10/10	10/16	10/14	10/13	10/12
Chanukkah - 1	W	IX - 25	12/11	12/17	12/16	12/14	12/13	12/12	12/18	12/16	12/15	12/14
Chodesh – Winter	Tu	IX - 31	12/17	12/23	12/22	12/20	12/19	12/18	12/24	12/22	12/21	12/20
Chanukkah - 8	W	X - 1	12/18	12/24	12/23	12/21	12/20	12/19	12/25	12/23	12/22	12/21

Appendix 3 – Gregorian Dates for Zadokite Events Through 2100

Special Event	Week Day	Zadokite Date	Gregorian 2051	Gregorian 2052	Gregorian 2053	Gregorian 2054	Gregorian 2055	Gregorian 2056	Gregorian 2057	Gregorian 2058	Gregorian 2059	Gregorian 2060
Purim	Sa	XII - 14	3/4	3/2	3/1	3/7	3/6	3/4	3/3	3/2	3/1	3/6
Shushan Purim	Su	XII - 15	3/5	3/3	3/2	3/8	3/7	3/5	3/4	3/3	3/2	3/7
Chodesh – Spring	Tu	XII - 31	3/21	3/19	3/18	3/24	3/23	3/21	3/20	3/19	3/18	3/23
New Year	W	I - 1	3/22	3/20	3/26	3/25	3/24	3/22	3/21	3/20	3/26	3/24
Passover	Tu	I - 14	4/4	4/2	4/8	4/7	4/6	4/4	4/3	4/2	4/8	4/6
Unleavened Br - 1	W	I - 15	4/5	4/3	4/9	4/8	4/7	4/5	4/4	4/3	4/9	4/7
Unleavened Br - 7	Tu	I - 21	4/11	4/9	4/15	4/14	4/13	4/11	4/10	4/9	4/15	4/13
Wave 1st Fruits	Su	I - 26	4/16	4/14	4/20	4/19	4/18	4/16	4/15	4/14	4/20	4/18
Pentecost	Su	III - 15	6/4	6/2	6/8	6/7	6/6	6/4	6/3	6/2	6/8	6/6
Chodesh – Summer	Tu	III - 31	6/20	6/18	6/24	6/23	6/22	6/20	6/19	6/18	6/24	6/22
Chodesh - Fall	Tu	VI - 31	9/19	9/17	9/23	9/22	9/21	9/19	9/18	9/17	9/23	9/21
Trumpets	W	VII - 1	9/20	9/18	9/24	9/23	9/22	9/20	9/19	9/18	9/24	9/22
Atonement	F	VII - 10	9/29	9/27	10/3	10/2	10/1	9/29	9/28	9/27	10/3	10/1
Tabernacles - 1	W	VII - 15	10/4	10/2	10/8	10/7	10/6	10/4	10/3	10/2	10/8	10/6
Tabernacles - 8	W	VII - 22	10/11	10/9	10/15	10/14	10/13	10/11	10/10	10/9	10/15	10/13
Chanukkah - 1	W	IX - 25	12/13	12/11	12/17	12/16	12/15	12/13	12/12	12/11	12/17	12/15
Chodesh – Winter	Tu	IX - 31	12/19	12/17	12/23	12/22	12/21	12/19	12/18	12/17	12/23	12/21
Chanukkah - 8	W	X - 1	12/20	12/18	12/24	12/23	12/22	12/20	12/19	12/18	12/24	12/22

Appendix 3 – Gregorian Dates for Zadokite Events Through 2100

Special Event	Week Day	Zadokite Date	Gregorian 2061	Gregorian 2062	Gregorian 2063	Gregorian 2064	Gregorian 2065	Gregorian 2066	Gregorian 2067	Gregorian 2068	Gregorian 2069	Gregorian 2070
Purim	Sa	XII - 14	3/5	3/4	3/3	3/1	3/7	3/6	3/5	3/3	3/2	3/1
Shushan Purim	Su	XII - 15	3/6	3/5	3/4	3/2	3/8	3/7	3/6	3/4	3/3	3/2
Chodesh – Spring	Tu	XII - 31	3/22	3/21	3/20	3/18	3/24	3/23	3/22	3/20	3/19	3/18
New Year	W	I - 1	3/23	3/22	3/21	3/26	3/25	3/24	3/23	3/21	3/20	3/26
Passover	Tu	I - 14	4/5	4/4	4/3	4/8	4/7	4/6	4/5	4/3	4/2	4/8
Unleavened Br - 1	W	I - 15	4/6	4/5	4/4	4/9	4/8	4/7	4/6	4/4	4/3	4/9
Unleavened Br - 7	Tu	I - 21	4/12	4/11	4/10	4/15	4/14	4/13	4/12	4/10	4/9	4/15
Wave 1st Fruits	Su	I - 26	4/17	4/16	4/15	4/20	4/19	4/18	4/17	4/15	4/14	4/20
Pentecost	Su	III - 15	6/5	6/4	6/3	6/8	6/7	6/6	6/5	6/3	6/2	6/8
Chodesh – Summer	Tu	III - 31	6/21	6/20	6/19	6/24	6/23	6/22	6/21	6/19	6/18	6/24
Chodesh - Fall	Tu	VI - 31	9/20	9/19	9/18	9/23	9/22	9/21	9/20	9/18	9/17	9/23
Trumpets	W	VII - 1	9/21	9/20	9/19	9/24	9/23	9/22	9/21	9/19	9/18	9/24
Atonement	F	VII - 10	9/30	9/29	9/28	10/3	10/2	10/1	9/30	9/28	9/27	10/3
Tabernacles - 1	W	VII - 15	10/5	10/4	10/3	10/8	10/7	10/6	10/5	10/3	10/2	10/8
Tabernacles - 8	W	VII - 22	10/12	10/11	10/10	10/15	10/14	10/13	10/12	10/10	10/9	10/15
Chanukkah - 1	W	IX - 25	12/14	12/13	12/12	12/17	12/16	12/15	12/14	12/12	12/11	12/17
Chodesh – Winter	Tu	IX - 31	12/20	12/19	12/18	12/23	12/22	12/21	12/20	12/18	12/17	12/23
Chanukkah - 8	W	X - 1	12/21	12/20	12/19	12/24	12/23	12/22	12/21	12/19	12/18	12/24

Appendix 3 – Gregorian Dates for Zadokite Events Through 2100

Special Event	Week Day	Zadokite Date	Gregorian 2071	Gregorian 2072	Gregorian 2073	Gregorian 2074	Gregorian 2075	Gregorian 2076	Gregorian 2077	Gregorian 2078	Gregorian 2079	Gregorian 2080
Purim	Sa	XII - 14	3/7	3/5	3/4	3/3	3/2	2/29	3/6	3/5	3/4	3/2
Shushan Purim	Su	XII - 15	3/8	3/6	3/5	3/4	3/3	3/1	3/7	3/6	3/5	3/3
Chodesh – Spring	Tu	XII - 31	3/24	3/22	3/21	3/20	3/19	3/17	3/23	3/22	3/21	3/19
New Year	W	I - 1	3/25	3/23	3/22	3/21	3/20	3/25	3/24	3/23	3/22	3/20
Passover	Tu	I - 14	4/7	4/5	4/4	4/3	4/2	4/7	4/6	4/5	4/4	4/2
Unleavened Br - 1	W	I - 15	4/8	4/6	4/5	4/4	4/3	4/8	4/7	4/6	4/5	4/3
Unleavened Br - 7	Tu	I - 21	4/14	4/12	4/11	4/10	4/9	4/14	4/13	4/12	4/11	4/9
Wave 1st Fruits	Su	I - 26	4/19	4/17	4/16	4/15	4/14	4/19	4/18	4/17	4/16	4/14
Pentecost	Su	III - 15	6/7	6/5	6/4	6/3	6/2	6/7	6/6	6/5	6/4	6/2
Chodesh – Summer	Tu	III - 31	6/23	6/21	6/20	6/19	6/18	6/23	6/22	6/21	6/20	6/18
Chodesh - Fall	Tu	VI - 31	9/22	9/20	9/19	9/18	9/17	9/22	9/21	9/20	9/19	9/17
Trumpets	W	VII - 1	9/23	9/21	9/20	9/19	9/18	9/23	9/22	9/21	9/20	9/18
Atonement	F	VII - 10	10/2	9/30	9/29	9/28	9/27	10/2	10/1	9/30	9/29	9/27
Tabernacles - 1	W	VII - 15	10/7	10/5	10/4	10/3	10/2	10/7	10/6	10/5	10/4	10/2
Tabernacles - 8	W	VII - 22	10/14	10/12	10/11	10/10	10/9	10/14	10/13	10/12	10/11	10/9
Chanukkah - 1	W	IX - 25	12/16	12/14	12/13	12/12	12/11	12/16	12/15	12/14	12/13	12/11
Chodesh – Winter	Tu	IX - 31	12/22	12/20	12/19	12/18	12/17	12/22	12/21	12/20	12/19	12/17
Chanukkah - 8	W	X - 1	12/23	12/21	12/20	12/19	12/18	12/23	12/22	12/21	12/20	12/18

Appendix 3 – Gregorian Dates for Zadokite Events Through 2100

Special Event	Week Day	Zadokite Date	Gregorian 2081	Gregorian 2082	Gregorian 2083	Gregorian 2084	Gregorian 2085	Gregorian 2086	Gregorian 2087	Gregorian 2088	Gregorian 2089	Gregorian 2090
Purim	Sa	XII - 14	3/1	3/7	3/6	3/4	3/3	3/2	3/1	3/6	3/5	3/4
Shushan Purim	Su	XII - 15	3/2	3/8	3/7	3/5	3/4	3/3	3/2	3/7	3/6	3/5
Chodesh – Spring	Tu	XII - 31	3/18	3/24	3/23	3/21	3/20	3/19	3/18	3/23	3/22	3/21
New Year	W	I - 1	3/26	3/25	3/24	3/22	3/21	3/20	3/26	3/24	3/23	3/22
Passover	Tu	I - 14	4/8	4/7	4/6	4/4	4/3	4/2	4/8	4/6	4/5	4/4
Unleavened Br - 1	W	I - 15	4/9	4/8	4/7	4/5	4/4	4/3	4/9	4/7	4/6	4/5
Unleavened Br - 7	Tu	I - 21	4/15	4/14	4/13	4/11	4/10	4/9	4/15	4/13	4/12	4/11
Wave 1st Fruits	Su	I - 26	4/20	4/19	4/18	4/16	4/15	4/14	4/20	4/18	4/17	4/16
Pentecost	Su	III - 15	6/8	6/7	6/6	6/4	6/3	6/2	6/8	6/6	6/5	6/4
Chodesh – Summer	Tu	III - 31	6/24	6/23	6/22	6/20	6/19	6/18	6/24	6/22	6/21	6/20
Chodesh – Fall	Tu	VI - 31	9/23	9/22	9/21	9/19	9/18	9/17	9/23	9/21	9/20	9/19
Trumpets	W	VII - 1	9/24	9/23	9/22	9/20	9/19	9/18	9/24	9/22	9/21	9/20
Atonement	F	VII - 10	10/3	10/2	10/1	9/29	9/28	9/27	10/3	10/1	9/30	9/29
Tabernacles - 1	W	VII - 15	10/8	10/7	10/6	10/4	10/3	10/2	10/8	10/6	10/5	10/4
Tabernacles - 8	W	VII - 22	10/15	10/14	10/13	10/11	10/10	10/9	10/15	10/13	10/12	10/11
Chanukkah - 1	W	IX - 25	12/17	12/16	12/15	12/13	12/12	12/11	12/17	12/15	12/14	12/13
Chodesh – Winter	Tu	IX - 31	12/23	12/22	12/21	12/19	12/18	12/17	12/23	12/21	12/20	12/19
Chanukkah - 8	W	X - 1	12/24	12/23	12/22	12/20	12/19	12/18	12/24	12/22	12/21	12/20

Appendix 3 – Gregorian Dates for Zadokite Events Through 2100

Special Event	Week Day	Zadokite Date	Gregorian 2091	Gregorian 2092	Gregorian 2093	Gregorian 2094	Gregorian 2095	Gregorian 2096	Gregorian 2097	Gregorian 2098	Gregorian 2099	Gregorian 2100
Purim	Sa	XII - 14	3/3	3/1	3/7	3/6	3/5	3/3	3/2	3/1	3/7	3/6
Shushan Purim	Su	XII - 15	3/4	3/2	3/8	3/7	3/6	3/4	3/3	3/2	3/8	3/7
Chodesh – Spring	Tu	XII - 31	3/20	3/18	3/24	3/23	3/22	3/20	3/19	3/18	3/24	3/23
New Year	W	I - 1	3/21	3/26	3/25	3/24	3/23	3/21	3/20	3/26	3/25	3/24
Passover	Tu	I - 14	4/3	4/8	4/7	4/6	4/5	4/3	4/2	4/8	4/7	4/6
Unleavened Br - 1	W	I - 15	4/4	4/9	4/8	4/7	4/6	4/4	4/3	4/9	4/8	4/7
Unleavened Br - 7	Tu	I - 21	4/10	4/15	4/14	4/13	4/12	4/10	4/9	4/15	4/14	4/13
Wave 1st Fruits	Su	I - 26	4/15	4/20	4/19	4/18	4/17	4/15	4/14	4/20	4/19	4/18
Pentecost	Su	III - 15	6/3	6/8	6/7	6/6	6/5	6/3	6/2	6/8	6/7	6/6
Chodesh – Summer	Tu	III - 31	6/19	6/24	6/23	6/22	6/21	6/19	6/18	6/24	6/23	6/22
Chodesh - Fall	Tu	VI - 31	9/18	9/23	9/22	9/21	9/20	9/18	9/17	9/23	9/22	9/21
Trumpets	W	VII - 1	9/19	9/24	9/23	9/22	9/21	9/19	9/18	9/24	9/23	9/22
Atonement	F	VII - 10	9/28	10/3	10/2	10/1	9/30	9/28	9/27	10/3	10/2	10/1
Tabernacles - 1	W	VII - 15	10/3	10/8	10/7	10/6	10/5	10/3	10/2	10/8	10/7	10/6
Tabernacles - 8	W	VII - 22	10/10	10/15	10/14	10/13	10/12	10/10	10/9	10/15	10/14	10/13
Chanukkah - 1	W	IX - 25	12/12	12/17	12/16	12/15	12/14	12/12	12/11	12/17	12/16	12/15
Chodesh – Winter	Tu	IX - 31	12/18	12/23	12/22	12/21	12/20	12/18	12/17	12/23	12/22	12/21
Chanukkah - 8	W	X - 1	12/19	12/24	12/23	12/22	12/21	12/19	12/18	12/24	12/23	12/22

Appendix 4 – Seasonal Change Data

This chart provides Jerusalem equinox, solstice, and sunset data. In Hebraic rendering, the new day begins at sundown, so if the equinox occurs after sundown, the date that counts as the equinox date advances by one day. Therefore, if the Equinox falls before sundown on a weekday 4 (Wednesday), the new year begins on that day. However if it falls after sundown on a weekday 4, it is actually counted as being a weekday 5, and the new year would begin on the following Weekday 4 (Wednesday). Considering the sundown criterion, the day that is actually counted as the Vernal Equinox date each year for purposes of calendar calculation is shown for you in the final column. If that date is a weekday 4 (Wednesday), the new year will start that day. If not, simply advance to the next weekday 4 (Wednesday) and begin the new year on that date, adding the extra week as needed.

Legend: All times are for Jerusalem and time data is recorded in military time. (See Appendix 7 for help with military time.)
SD = Sundown; VE = Vernal Equinox; SS = Summer Solstice; AE = Autumnal Equinox; WS = Winter Solstice

VE Date	VE Time	SD Time	SS Date	SS Time	SD Time	AE Date	AE Tie	SD Time	WS Date	WS Time	SD Time	Day Counted As VE Date
03/20/17	12:29	17:50	06/21/17	07:24	19:47	09/22/17	23:02	18:35	12/21/17	18:28	16:39	03/20/17
03/20/18	18:15	17:51	06/21/18	13:07	19:47	09/23/18	04:54	18:34	12/22/18	00:23	16:39	03/21/18
03/20/19	23:59	17:50	06/21/19	18:54	19:47	09/23/19	10:50	18:35	12/22/19	06:19	16:39	03/21/19
03/20/20	05:50	17:50	06/21/20	00:44	19:47	09/22/20	16:31	18:35	12/21/20	12:02	16:39	03/20/20
03/20/21	11:37	17:50	06/21/21	06:32	19:47	09/22/21	22:21	18:35	12/21/21	17:59	16:39	03/20/21
03/20/22	17:33	17:50	06/21/22	12:14	19:47	09/23/22	04:04	18:34	12/21/22	23:48	16:39	03/20/22
03/20/23	23:24	17:50	06/21/23	17:58	19:47	09/23/23	09:50	18:35	12/22/23	05:27	16:39	03/21/23
03/20/24	05:06	17:50	06/20/24	23:51	19:47	09/22/24	15:43	18:35	12/21/24	11:20	16:39	03/20/24
03/20/25	11:01	17:50	06/21/25	05:42	19:47	09/22/25	17:19	18:35	12/21/25	17:03	16:39	03/20/25
03/20/26	16:46	17:50	06/21/26	11:24	19:47	09/23/26	03:05	18:34	12/21/26	22:50	16:39	03/20/26
03/20/27	22:25	17:50	06/21/27	17:11	19:47	09/23/27	09:02	18:35	12/22/27	04:42	16:39	03/21/27
03/20/28	04:17	17:50	06/20/28	23:02	19:47	09/22/28	14:45	18:35	12/21/28	10:20	16:39	03/20/28
03/20/29	10:02	17:50	06/21/29	04:48	19:47	09/22/29	20:38	18:35	12/21/29	16:14	16:39	03/20/29
03/20/30	15:52	17:50	06/21/30	10:31	19:47	09/23/30	02:27	18:34	12/21/30	22:09	16:39	03/20/30
03/20/31	21:41	17:50	06/21/31	16:17	19:47	09/23/31	08:15	18:34	12/22/31	03:55	16:39	03/21/31
03/20/32	03:22	17:50	06/20/32	22:09	19:47	09/22/32	14:11	18:35	12/21/32	09:56	16:39	03/20/32

Appendix 4 – Seasonal Change Data

VE Date & Time		SD Time	SS Date & Time		SD Time	AE Date & Time		SD Time	WS Date & Time		SD Time	Day Counted As VE Date
03/20/33	09:23	17:50	06/21/33	04:01	19:47	09/22/33	19:51	18:35	12/21/33	15:46	16:38	03/20/33
03/20/34	15:17	17:50	06/21/34	09:44	19:47	09/23/34	01:39	18:34	12/21/34	21:34	16:39	03/20/34
03/20/35	17:02	17:50	06/21/35	15:33	19:47	09/23/35	07:39	18:34	12/22/35	03:31	16:39	03/20/35
03/20/36	03:03	17:50	06/20/36	17:32	19:47	09/22/36	13:23	18:35	12/21/36	09:13	16:39	03/20/36
03/20/37	08:50	17:50	06/21/37	03:22	19:47	09/22/37	19:13	18:35	12/21/37	15:08	16:39	03/20/37
03/20/38	14:41	17:50	06/21/38	09:09	19:47	09/23/38	01:02	18:34	12/21/38	21:02	16:39	03/20/38
03/20/39	20:32	17:50	06/21/39	14:57	19:47	09/23/39	06:49	18:34	12/22/39	02:40	16:39	03/21/39
03/20/40	02:11	17:50	06/20/40	20:46	19:47	09/22/40	12:45	18:35	12/21/40	08:33	16:39	03/20/40
03/20/41	08:07	17:50	06/21/41	02:36	19:47	09/22/41	18:26	18:35	12/21/41	14:18	16:39	03/20/41
03/20/42	13:53	17:50	06/21/42	08:16	19:47	09/23/42	00:11	18:34	12/21/42	20:04	16:39	03/20/42
03/20/43	19:28	17:50	06/21/43	13:58	19:47	09/23/43	06:07	18:34	12/22/43	02:01	16:39	03/21/43
03/20/43	19:28	17:50	06/21/43	13:58	19:47	09/23/43	06:07	18:34	12/22/43	02:01	16:39	03/21/43
03/20/44	01:20	17:50	06/20/44	19:51	19:47	09/22/44	11:48	18:35	12/21/44	07:43	16:39	03/20/44
03/20/45	07:07	17:50	06/21/45	01:34	19:47	09/22/45	17:33	18:35	12/21/45	13:35	16:39	03/20/45
03/20/46	12:58	17:50	06/21/46	07:14	19:47	09/22/46	23:21	18:35	12/21/46	19:26	16:39	03/20/46
03/20/47	18:52	17:50	06/21/47	13:03	19:47	09/23/47	05:08	18:34	12/22/47	01:07	16:39	03/21/47
03/20/48	00:34	17:50	06/20/48	18:54	19:47	09/22/48	11:00	18:35	12/21/48	07:02	16:39	03/20/48
03/20/49	06:28	17:50	06/21/49	00:47	19:47	09/22/49	16:42	18:35	12/21/49	12:52	16:39	03/20/49
03/20/50	12:19	17:50	06/21/50	06:33	19:47	09/22/50	22:28	18:35	12/21/50	18:38	16:39	03/20/50
03/20/51	17:59	17:50	06/21/51	12:18	19:47	09/23/51	04:27	18:34	12/22/51	00:34	16:39	03/21/51
03/19/52	23:56	17:50	06/20/52	06:16	19:47	09/22/52	10:15	18:35	12/21/52	06:17	16:39	03/20/52
03/20/53	05:47	17:50	06/21/53	00:04	19:47	09/22/53	16:06	18:35	12/21/53	12:10	16:39	03/20/53
03/20/54	11:34	17:50	06/21/54	05:47	19:47	09/22/54	21:59	18:35	12/21/54	10:10	16:39	03/20/54
03/20/55	17:28	17:50	06/21/55	11:40	19:47	09/23/55	03:48	18:34	12/21/55	23:55	16:39	03/20/55
03/19/56	23:11	17:50	06/20/56	17:28	19:47	09/22/56	09:39	18:35	12/21/56	05:51	16:39	03/20/56
03/20/57	05:08	17:50	06/20/57	23:19	19:47	09/22/57	15:23	18:35	12/21/57	11:43	16:39	03/20/57
03/20/58	11:05	17:50	06/21/58	05:04	19:47	09/22/58	21:08	18:35	12/21/58	17:25	16:39	03/20/58
03/20/59	16:44	17:50	06/21/59	10:47	19:47	09/23/59	03:03	18:34	12/21/59	00:18	16:39	03/20/59
03/19/60	22:38	17:50	06/20/60	16:45	19:47	09/22/60	08:48	18:35	12/21/60	05:01	16:39	03/20/60

Appendix 4 – Seasonal Change Data

VE Date & Time		SD Time	SS Date & Time		SD Time	AE Date & Time		SD Time	WS Date & Time		SD Time	Day Counted As VE Date
03/20/61	04:26	17:50	06/20/61	22:32	19:47	09/22/61	14:31	18:35	12/21/61	10:49	16:39	03/20/61
03/20/62	10:07	17:50	06/21/06	04:11	19:47	09/22/62	20:20	18:35	12/21/62	16:42	16:39	03/20/62
03/20/63	15:59	17:50	06/21/63	10:02	19:47	09/23/63	02:08	18:34	12/21/63	22:21	16:39	03/20/63
03/19/64	21:38	17:50	06/20/64	15:45	19:47	09/22/64	07:57	18:34	12/21/64	04:09	16:39	03/20/64
03/20/65	03:28	17:50	06/20/65	21:32	19:47	09/22/65	13:42	18:35	12/21/65	10:00	16:39	03/20/65
03/20/66	09:20	17:50	06/21/66	03:16	19:47	09/22/66	19:27	18:35	12/21/66	15:45	16:39	03/20/66
03/20/67	14:53	17:50	06/21/67	08:56	19:47	09/23/67	01:19	18:34	12/21/67	17:43	16:39	03/20/67
03/19/68	20:49	17:50	06/20/68	14:53	19:47	09/22/68	07:07	18:34	12/21/68	03:32	16:39	03/20/68
03/20/69	02:45	17:50	06/20/69	20:41	19:47	09/22/69	12:51	18:35	12/21/69	09:22	16:39	03/20/69
03/20/70	08:34	17:50	06/21/70	02:22	19:47	09/22/70	18:45	18:35	12/21/70	15:19	16:39	03/20/70
03/20/71	14:34	17:50	06/21/71	08:21	19:47	09/23/71	00:37	18:34	12/21/71	21:04	16:39	03/20/71
03/19/72	20:21	17:50	06/20/72	14:13	19:47	09/22/72	06:27	18:34	12/21/72	02:56	16:39	03/20/72
03/20/73	02:13	17:50	06/20/73	20:07	19:47	09/22/73	12:15	18:35	12/21/73	08:50	16:39	03/20/73
03/20/74	08:09	17:50	06/21/74	01:58	19:47	09/22/74	18:03	18:35	12/21/74	14:35	16:39	03/20/74
03/20/75	13:46	17:50	06/21/75	07:40	19:47	09/22/75	23:59	18:35	12/21/75	20:27	16:39	03/20/75
03/19/76	19:39	17:50	06/20/76	13:36	19:47	09/22/76	05:50	18:34	12/21/76	02:13	16:39	03/20/76
03/20/77	01:31	17:50	06/20/77	19:23	19:47	09/22/77	11:36	18:35	12/21/77	08:01	16:39	03/20/77
03/20/78	07:11	17:50	06/21/78	00:58	19:47	09/22/78	17:24	18:35	12/21/78	13:58	16:39	03/20/78
03/20/79	13:00	17:50	06/21/79	06:49	19:47	09/22/79	23:13	18:35	12/21/79	19:44	16:39	03/20/79
03/19/80	18:44	17:50	06/20/80	12:34	19:47	09/22/80	04:56	18:34	12/21/80	01:33	16:39	03/20/80
03/20/81	00:34	17:50	06/20/81	18:16	19:47	09/22/81	10:37	18:35	12/21/81	07:22	16:39	03/20/81
03/20/82	06:30	17:50	06/21/82	00:03	19:47	09/22/82	16:23	18:35	12/21/82	13:04	16:39	03/20/82
03/20/83	12:10	17:50	06/21/83	05:44	19:47	09/22/83	22:11	18:35	12/21/83	18:53	16:39	03/20/83
03/19/84	17:59	17:50	06/20/84	11:40	19:47	09/22/84	03:59	18:34	12/21/84	00:41	16:39	03/20/84
03/19/85	23:53	17:50	06/20/85	17:33	19:47	09/22/85	09:43	18:35	12/21/85	06:28	16:39	03/20/85
03/20/86	05:35	17:50	06/20/86	23:09	19:47	09/22/86	15:32	18:35	12/21/86	12:22	16:39	03/20/86
03/20/87	11:28	17:50	06/21/87	05:06	19:47	09/22/87	21:28	18:35	12/21/87	18:08	16:39	03/20/87
03/19/88	17:17	17:50	06/20/88	10:56	19:47	09/22/88	03:18	18:34	12/20/88	23:56	16:39	03/19/88
03/19/89	23:06	17:50	06/20/89	16:43	19:47	09/22/89	09:07	18:35	12/21/89	05:52	16:39	03/20/89

Appendix 4 – Seasonal Change Data

VE Date & Time		SD Time	SS Date & Time		SD Time	AE Date & Time		SD Time	WS Date & Time		SD Time	Day Counted As VE Date
03/20/90	05:02	17:50	06/20/90	22:36	19:47	09/22/90	14:59	18:35	12/21/90	11:43	16:39	03/20/90
03/20/91	10:42	17:50	06/21/91	04:19	19:47	09/22/91	20:51	18:35	12/21/91	17:38	16:39	03/20/91
03/19/92	16:33	17:50	06/20/92	10:15	19:47	09/22/92	02:42	18:34	12/20/92	23:32	16:39	03/19/92
03/19/93	22:34	17:50	06/20/93	16:07	19:47	09/22/93	08:29	18:35	12/21/93	05:21	16:39	03/20/93
03/20/94	04:21	17:50	06/20/94	21:42	19:47	09/22/94	14:16	18:35	12/21/94	11:13	16:39	03/20/94
03/20/95	10:15	17:50	06/21/95	03:39	19:47	09/22/95	20:11	18:35	12/21/95	17:01	16:39	03/20/95
03/19/96	16:03	17:50	06/20/96	09:31	19:47	09/22/96	01:55	18:34	12/20/96	22:46	16:39	03/19/96
03/19/97	21:48	17:50	06/20/97	15:13	19:47	09/22/97	07:36	18:34	12/21/97	04:37	16:39	03/20/97
03/20/98	03:40	17:50	06/20/98	21:03	19:47	09/22/98	13:24	18:35	12/21/98	10:21	16:39	03/20/98
03/20/99	09:17	17:50	06/21/99	02:41	19:47	09/22/99	19:11	18:35	12/21/99	16:04	16:39	03/20/99
03/20/00	21:04	17:50	06/21/00	14:32	19:47	09/23/00	07:00	18:34	12/22/00	03:51	16:39	03/21/00

In order to know when a weekday 4 (Wednesday) will be on the Gregorian calendar, it would be helpful to know what the calendar for future years would look like. There are 14 schemata, which will be found under Appendix 6. The information in this appendix will show you which Gregorian years align to each of the 14 schemata. Then you can use the appropriate schema to see what the calendar will look like for any particular year.

Current Year	Schema Number	Years that Share a Common Schema
2017	1	2023, 2034, 2045, 2051, 2062, 2073, 2079, 2090
2018	2	2029, 2035, 2046, 2057, 2063, 2074, 2085, 2091
2019	3	2030, 2041, 2047, 2058, 2069, 2075, 2086, 2097
2020	8	2048, 2076
2021	4	2027, 2038, 2049, 2055, 2066, 2077, 2083, 2094, 2100
2022	5	2033, 2039, 2050, 2061, 2067, 2078, 2089, 2095
2023	1	2017, 2034, 2045, 2051, 2062, 2073, 2079, 2090
2024	9	2052, 2080
2025	6	2031, 2042, 2053, 2059, 2070, 2081, 2087, 2098
2026	7	2037, 2043, 2054, 2065, 2071, 2082, 2093, 2099
2027	4	2021, 2038, 2049, 2055, 2066, 2077, 2083, 2094, 2100
2028	10	2056, 2084
2029	2	2018, 2035, 2046, 2057, 2063, 2074, 2085, 2091
2030	3	2019, 2041, 2047, 2058, 2069, 2075, 2086, 2097
2031	6	2025, 2042, 2053, 2059, 2070, 2081, 2087, 2098
2032	11	2060, 2088
2033	5	2022, 2039, 2050, 2061, 2067, 2078, 2089, 2095
2034	1	2017, 2023, 2045, 2051, 2062, 2073, 2079, 2090
2035	2	2018, 2029, 2046, 2057, 2063, 2074, 2085, 2091
2036	12	2064, 2092
2037	7	2026, 2043, 2054, 2065, 2071, 2082, 2093, 2099
2038	4	2021, 2027, 2049, 2055, 2066, 2077, 2083, 2094, 2100
2039	5	2022, 2033, 2050, 2061, 2067, 2078, 2089, 2095
2040	13	2068, 2096
2041	3	2019, 2030, 2047, 2058, 2069, 2075, 2086, 2097
2042	6	2025, 2031, 2053, 2059, 2070, 2081, 2087, 2098
2043	7	2026, 2037, 2054, 2065, 2071, 2082, 2093, 2099
2044	14	2072
2045	1	2017, 2023, 2034, 2051, 2062, 2073, 2079, 2090
2046	2	2018, 2029, 2035, 2057, 2063, 2074, 2085, 2091
2047	3	2019, 2030, 2041, 2058, 2069, 2075, 2086, 2097
2048	8	2020, 2076
2049	4	2021, 2027, 2038, 2055, 2066, 2077, 2083, 2094, 2100
2050	5	2022, 2033, 2039, 2061, 2067, 2078, 2089, 2095
2051	1	2017, 2023, 2034, 2045, 2062, 2073, 2079, 2090
2052	9	2024, 2080

Current Year	Schema Number	Years that Share a Common Schema
2053	6	2025, 2031, 2042, 2059, 2070, 2081, 2087, 2098
2054	7	2026, 2037, 2043, 2065, 2071, 2082, 2093, 2099
2055	4	2021, 2027, 2038, 2049, 2066, 2077, 2083, 2094, 2100
2056	10	2028, 2084
2057	2	2018, 2029, 2035, 2046, 2063, 2074, 2085, 2091
2058	3	2019, 2030, 2041, 2047, 2069, 2075, 2086, 2097
2059	6	2025, 2031, 2042, 2053, 2070, 2081, 2087, 2098
2060	11	2032, 2088
2061	5	2022, 2033, 2039, 2050, 2067, 2078, 2089, 2095
2062	1	2017, 2023, 2034, 2045, 2051, 2073, 2079, 2090
2063	2	2018, 2029, 2035, 2046, 2057, 2074, 2085, 2091
2064	12	2036, 2092
2065	7	2026, 2037, 2043, 2054, 2071, 2082, 2093, 2099
2066	4	2021, 2027, 2038, 2049, 2055, 2077, 2083, 2094, 2100
2067	5	2022, 2033, 2039, 2050, 2061, 2078, 2089, 2095
2068	13	2040, 2096
2069	3	2019, 2030, 2041, 2047, 2058, 2075, 2086, 2097
2070	6	2025, 2031, 2042, 2053, 2059, 2081, 2087, 2098
2071	7	2026, 2037, 2043, 2054, 2065, 2082, 2093, 2099
2072	14	2044
2073	1	2017, 2023, 2034, 2045, 2051, 2062, 2079, 2090
2074	2	2018, 2029, 2035, 2046, 2057, 2063, 2085, 2091
2075	3	2019, 2030, 2041, 2047, 2058, 2069, 2086, 2097
2076	8	2020, 2048
2077	4	2021, 2027, 2038, 2049, 2055, 2066, 2083, 2094, 2100
2078	5	2022, 2033, 2039, 2050, 2061, 2067, 2089, 2095
2079	1	2017, 2023, 2034, 2045, 2051, 2062, 2073, 2090
2080	9	2024, 2052
2081	6	2025, 2031, 2042, 2053, 2059, 2070, 2087, 2098
2082	7	2026, 2037, 2043, 2054, 2065, 2071, 2093, 2099
2083	4	2021, 2027, 2038, 2049, 2055, 2066, 2077, 2094, 2100
2084	10	2028, 2056
2085	2	2018, 2029, 2035, 2046, 2057, 2063, 2074, 2091
2086	3	2019, 2030, 2041, 2047, 2058, 2069, 2075, 2097
2087	6	2025, 2031, 2042, 2053, 2059, 2070, 2081, 2098
2088	11	2032, 2060
2089	5	2022, 2033, 2039, 2050, 2061, 2067, 2078, 2095
2090	1	2017, 2023, 2034, 2045, 2051, 2062, 2073, 2079
2091	2	2018, 2029, 2035, 2046, 2057, 2063, 2074, 2085
2092	12	2036, 2064
2093	7	2026, 2037, 2043, 2054, 2065, 2071, 2082, 2099
2094	4	2021, 2027, 2038, 2049, 2055, 2066, 2077, 2083, 2100

Appendix 5 – Gregorian Calendar Repetition Schemata		
Current	Schema	Years that Share
Year	Number	a Common Schema
2095	5	2022, 2033, 2039, 2050, 2061, 2067, 2078, 2089
2096	13	2040, 2068
2097	3	2019, 2030, 2041, 2047, 2058, 2069, 2075, 2086
2098	6	2025, 2031, 2042, 2053, 2059, 2070, 2081, 2087
2099	7	2026, 2037, 2043, 2054, 2065, 2071, 2082, 2093
2100	4	2021, 2027, 2038, 2049, 2055, 2066, 2077, 2083, 2094

Appendix 6 – The 14 Schemata for Gregorian Calendar Years
The 14 schemata referenced in Appendix 5 are found in this Appendix. They will correspond to the data of Appendix 5 to allow you to see which weekdays will align to future dates on successive Gregorian calendar years. Please turn to the next page for the series of schemata.

Schema #1

JANUARY

S	M	T	W	T	F	S
1	2	3	4	5	6	7
8	9	10	11	12	13	14
15	16	17	18	19	20	21
22	23	24	25	26	27	28
29	30	31				

FEBRUARY

S	M	T	W	T	F	S
			1	2	3	4
5	6	7	8	9	10	11
12	13	14	15	16	17	18
19	20	21	22	23	24	25
26	27	28				

MARCH

S	M	T	W	T	F	S
			1	2	3	4
5	6	7	8	9	10	11
12	13	14	15	16	17	18
19	20	21	22	23	24	25
26	27	28	29	30	31	

APRIL

S	M	T	W	T	F	S
						1
2	3	4	5	6	7	8
9	10	11	12	13	14	15
16	17	18	19	20	21	22
23	24	25	26	27	28	29
30						

MAY

S	M	T	W	T	F	S
	1	2	3	4	5	6
7	8	9	10	11	12	13
14	15	16	17	18	19	20
21	22	23	24	25	26	27
28	29	30	31			

JUNE

S	M	T	W	T	F	S
				1	2	3
4	5	6	7	8	9	10
11	12	13	14	15	16	17
18	19	20	21	22	23	24
25	26	27	28	29	30	

JULY

S	M	T	W	T	F	S
						1
2	3	4	5	6	7	8
9	10	11	12	13	14	15
16	17	18	19	20	21	22
23	24	25	26	27	28	29
30	31					

AUGUST

S	M	T	W	T	F	S
		1	2	3	4	5
6	7	8	9	10	11	12
13	14	15	16	17	18	19
20	21	22	23	24	25	26
27	28	29	30	31		

SEPTEMBER

S	M	T	W	T	F	S
					1	2
3	4	5	6	7	8	9
10	11	12	13	14	15	16
17	18	19	20	21	22	23
24	25	26	27	28	29	30

OCTOBER

S	M	T	W	T	F	S
1	2	3	4	5	6	7
8	9	10	11	12	13	14
15	16	17	18	19	20	21
22	23	24	25	26	27	28
29	30	31				

NOVEMBER

S	M	T	W	T	F	S
			1	2	3	4
5	6	7	8	9	10	11
12	13	14	15	16	17	18
19	20	21	22	23	24	25
26	27	28	29	30		

DECEMBER

S	M	T	W	T	F	S
					1	2
3	4	5	6	7	8	9
10	11	12	13	14	15	16
17	18	19	20	21	22	23
24	25	26	27	28	29	30
31						

Schema #2

JANUARY

S	M	T	W	T	F	S
	1	2	3	4	5	6
7	8	9	10	11	12	13
14	15	16	17	18	19	20
21	22	23	24	25	26	27
28	29	30	31			

FEBRUARY

S	M	T	W	T	F	S
				1	2	3
4	5	6	7	8	9	10
11	12	13	14	15	16	17
18	19	20	21	22	23	24
25	26	27	28			

MARCH

S	M	T	W	T	F	S
				1	2	3
4	5	6	7	8	9	10
11	12	13	14	15	16	17
18	19	20	21	22	23	24
25	26	27	28	29	30	31

APRIL

S	M	T	W	T	F	S
1	2	3	4	5	6	7
8	9	10	11	12	13	14
15	16	17	18	19	20	21
22	23	24	25	26	27	28
29	30					

MAY

S	M	T	W	T	F	S
		1	2	3	4	5
6	7	8	9	10	11	12
13	14	15	16	17	18	19
20	21	22	23	24	25	26
27	28	29	30	31		

JUNE

S	M	T	W	T	F	S
					1	2
3	4	5	6	7	8	9
10	11	12	13	14	15	16
17	18	19	20	21	22	23
24	25	26	27	28	29	30

JULY

S	M	T	W	T	F	S
1	2	3	4	5	6	7
8	9	10	11	12	13	14
15	16	17	18	19	20	21
22	23	24	25	26	27	28
29	30	31				

AUGUST

S	M	T	W	T	F	S
			1	2	3	4
5	6	7	8	9	10	11
12	13	14	15	16	17	18
19	20	21	22	23	24	25
26	27	28	29	30	31	

SEPTEMBER

S	M	T	W	T	F	S
						1
2	3	4	5	6	7	8
9	10	11	12	13	14	15
16	17	18	19	20	21	22
23	24	25	26	27	28	29
30						

OCTOBER

S	M	T	W	T	F	S
	1	2	3	4	5	6
7	8	9	10	11	12	13
14	15	16	17	18	19	20
21	22	23	24	25	26	27
28	29	30	31			

NOVEMBER

S	M	T	W	T	F	S
				1	2	3
4	5	6	7	8	9	10
11	12	13	14	15	16	17
18	19	20	21	22	23	24
25	26	27	28	29	30	

DECEMBER

S	M	T	W	T	F	S
						1
2	3	4	5	6	7	8
9	10	11	12	13	14	15
16	17	18	19	20	21	22
23	24	25	26	27	28	29
30	31					

Schema #3

JANUARY

S	M	T	W	T	F	S
		1	2	3	4	5
6	7	8	9	10	11	12
13	14	15	16	17	18	19
20	21	22	23	24	25	26
27	28	29	30	31		

FEBRUARY

S	M	T	W	T	F	S
					1	2
3	4	5	6	7	8	9
10	11	12	13	14	15	16
17	18	19	20	21	22	23
24	25	26	27	28		

MARCH

S	M	T	W	T	F	S
					1	2
3	4	5	6	7	8	9
10	11	12	13	14	15	16
17	18	19	20	21	22	23
24	25	26	27	28	29	30
31						

APRIL

S	M	T	W	T	F	S
	1	2	3	4	5	6
7	8	9	10	11	12	13
14	15	16	17	18	19	20
21	22	23	24	25	26	27
28	29	30				

MAY

S	M	T	W	T	F	S
			1	2	3	4
5	6	7	8	9	10	11
12	13	14	15	16	17	18
19	20	21	22	23	24	25
26	27	28	29	30	31	

JUNE

S	M	T	W	T	F	S
						1
2	3	4	5	6	7	8
9	10	11	12	13	14	15
16	17	18	19	20	21	22
23	24	25	26	27	28	29
30						

JULY

S	M	T	W	T	F	S
	1	2	3	4	5	6
7	8	9	10	11	12	13
14	15	16	17	18	19	20
21	22	23	24	25	26	27
28	29	30	31			

AUGUST

S	M	T	W	T	F	S
				1	2	3
4	5	6	7	8	9	10
11	12	13	14	15	16	17
18	19	20	21	22	23	24
25	26	27	28	29	30	31

SEPTEMBER

S	M	T	W	T	F	S
1	2	3	4	5	6	7
8	9	10	11	12	13	14
15	16	17	18	19	20	21
22	23	24	25	26	27	28
29	30					

OCTOBER

S	M	T	W	T	F	S
		1	2	3	4	5
6	7	8	9	10	11	12
13	14	15	16	17	18	19
20	21	22	23	24	25	26
27	28	29	30	31		

NOVEMBER

S	M	T	W	T	F	S
					1	2
3	4	5	6	7	8	9
10	11	12	13	14	15	16
17	18	19	20	21	22	23
24	25	26	27	28	29	30

DECEMBER

S	M	T	W	T	F	S
1	2	3	4	5	6	7
8	9	10	11	12	13	14
15	16	17	18	19	20	21
22	23	24	25	26	27	28
29	30	31				

Schema #4

JANUARY

S	M	T	W	T	F	S
					1	2
3	4	5	6	7	8	9
10	11	12	13	14	15	16
17	18	19	20	21	22	23
24	25	26	27	28	29	30
31						

FEBRUARY

S	M	T	W	T	F	S
	1	2	3	4	5	6
7	8	9	10	11	12	13
14	15	16	17	18	19	20
21	22	23	24	25	26	27
28						

MARCH

S	M	T	W	T	F	S
	1	2	3	4	5	6
7	8	9	10	11	12	13
14	15	16	17	18	19	20
21	22	23	24	25	26	27
28	29	30	31			

APRIL

S	M	T	W	T	F	S
				1	2	3
4	5	6	7	8	9	10
11	12	13	14	15	16	17
18	19	20	21	22	23	24
25	26	27	28	29	30	

MAY

S	M	T	W	T	F	S
						1
5	6	7	8	9	10	11
12	13	14	15	16	17	18
19	20	21	22	23	24	25
26	27	28	29	30	31	

JUNE

S	M	T	W	T	F	S
	1	2	3	4	5	
6	7	8	9	10	11	12
13	14	15	16	17	18	19
20	21	22	23	24	25	26
27	28	29	30			

JULY

S	M	T	W	T	F	S
				1	2	3
4	5	6	7	8	9	10
11	12	13	14	15	16	17
18	19	20	21	22	23	24
25	26	27	28	29	30	31

AUGUST

S	M	T	W	T	F	S
1	2	3	4	5	6	7
8	9	10	11	12	13	14
15	16	17	18	19	20	21
22	23	24	25	26	27	28
29	30	31				

SEPTEMBER

S	M	T	W	T	F	S
			1	2	3	4
5	6	7	8	9	10	11
12	13	14	15	16	17	18
19	20	21	22	23	24	25
26	27	28	29	30		

OCTOBER

S	M	T	W	T	F	S
					1	2
3	4	5	6	7	8	9
10	11	12	13	14	15	16
17	18	19	20	21	22	23
24	25	26	27	28	29	30
31						

NOVEMBER

S	M	T	W	T	F	S
	1	2	3	4	5	6
7	8	9	10	11	12	13
14	15	16	17	18	19	20
21	22	23	24	25	26	27
28	29	30				

DECEMBER

S	M	T	W	T	F	S
			1	2	3	4
5	6	7	8	9	10	11
12	13	14	15	16	17	18
19	20	21	22	23	24	25
26	27	28	29	30	31	

Schema #5

JANUARY

S	M	T	W	T	F	S
						1
2	3	4	5	6	7	8
9	10	11	12	13	14	15
16	17	18	19	20	21	22
23	24	25	26	27	28	29
30	31					

FEBRUARY

S	M	T	W	T	F	S
		1	2	3	4	5
6	7	8	9	10	11	12
13	14	15	16	17	18	19
20	21	22	23	24	25	26
27	28					

MARCH

S	M	T	W	T	F	S
		1	2	3	4	5
6	7	8	9	10	11	12
13	14	15	16	17	18	19
20	21	22	23	24	25	26
27	28	29	30	31		

APRIL

S	M	T	W	T	F	S
					1	2
3	4	5	6	7	8	9
10	11	12	13	14	15	16
17	18	19	20	21	22	23
24	25	26	27	28	29	30

MAY

S	M	T	W	T	F	S
1	2	3	4	5	6	7
8	9	10	11	12	13	14
15	16	17	18	19	20	21
22	23	24	25	26	27	28
29	30	31				

JUNE

S	M	T	W	T	F	S
			1	2	3	4
5	6	7	8	9	10	11
12	13	14	15	16	17	18
19	20	21	22	23	24	25
26	27	28	29	50		

JULY

S	M	T	W	T	F	S
					1	2
3	4	5	6	7	8	9
10	11	12	13	14	15	16
17	18	19	20	21	22	23
24	25	26	27	28	29	30

AUGUST

S	M	T	W	T	F	S
	1	2	3	4	5	6
7	8	9	10	11	12	13
14	15	16	17	18	19	20
21	22	23	24	25	26	27
28	29	30	31			

SEPTEMBER

S	M	T	W	T	F	S
				1	2	3
4	5	6	7	8	9	10
11	12	13	14	15	16	17
18	19	20	21	22	23	24
25	26	27	28	29	30	

OCTOBER

S	M	T	W	T	F	S
						1
2	3	4	5	6	7	8
9	10	11	12	13	14	15
16	17	18	19	20	21	22
23	24	25	26	27	28	29
30	31					

NOVEMBER

S	M	T	W	T	F	S
		1	2	3	4	5
6	7	8	9	10	11	12
13	14	15	16	17	18	19
20	21	22	23	24	25	26
27	28	29	30			

DECEMBER

S	M	T	W	T	F	S
				1	2	3
4	5	6	7	8	9	10
11	12	13	14	15	16	17
18	19	20	21	22	23	24
25	26	27	28	29	30	31

Schema #6

JANUARY

S	M	T	W	T	F	S
			1	2	3	4
5	6	7	8	9	10	11
12	13	14	15	16	17	18
19	20	21	22	23	24	25
26	27	28	29	30	31	

FEBRUARY

S	M	T	W	T	F	S
						1
2	3	4	5	6	7	8
9	10	11	12	13	14	15
16	17	18	19	20	21	22
23	24	25	26	27	28	

MARCH

S	M	T	W	T	F	S
						1
2	3	4	5	6	7	8
9	10	11	12	13	14	15
16	17	18	19	20	21	22
23	24	25	26	27	28	29
30	31					

APRIL

S	M	T	W	T	F	S
		1	2	3	4	5
6	7	8	9	10	11	12
13	14	15	16	17	18	19
20	21	22	23	24	25	26
27	28	29	30			

MAY

S	M	T	W	T	F	S
				1	2	3
4	5	6	7	8	9	10
11	12	13	14	15	16	17
18	19	20	21	22	23	24
25	26	27	28	29	30	31

JUNE

S	M	T	W	T	F	S
1	2	3	4	5	6	7
8	9	10	11	12	13	14
15	16	17	18	19	20	21
22	23	24	25	26	27	28
29	30					

JULY

S	M	T	W	T	F	S
		1	2	3	4	5
6	7	8	9	10	11	12
13	14	15	16	17	18	19
20	21	22	23	24	25	26
27	28	29	30	31		

AUGUST

S	M	T	W	T	F	S
					1	2
3	4	5	6	7	8	9
10	11	12	13	14	15	16
17	18	19	20	21	22	23
24	25	26	27	28	29	30
31						

SEPTEMBER

S	M	T	W	T	F	S
	1	2	3	4	5	6
7	8	9	10	11	12	13
14	15	16	17	18	19	20
21	22	23	24	25	26	27
28	29	30				

OCTOBER

S	M	T	W	T	F	S
			1	2	3	4
5	6	7	8	9	10	11
12	13	14	15	16	17	18
19	20	21	22	23	24	25
26	27	28	29	30	31	

NOVEMBER

S	M	T	W	T	F	S
						1
2	3	4	5	6	7	8
9	10	11	12	13	14	15
16	17	18	19	20	21	22
23	24	25	26	27	28	29
30						

DECEMBER

S	M	T	W	T	F	S
	1	2	3	4	5	6
7	8	9	10	11	12	13
14	15	16	17	18	19	20
21	22	23	24	25	26	27
28	29	30	31			

Schema #7

JANUARY

S	M	T	W	T	F	S
				1	2	3
4	5	6	7	8	9	10
11	12	13	14	15	16	17
18	19	20	21	22	23	24
25	26	27	28	29	30	31

FEBRUARY

S	M	T	W	T	F	S
1	2	3	4	5	6	7
8	9	10	11	12	13	14
15	16	17	18	19	20	21
22	23	24	25	26	27	28

MARCH

S	M	T	W	T	F	S
1	2	3	4	5	6	7
8	9	10	11	12	13	14
15	16	17	18	19	20	21
22	23	24	25	26	27	28
29	30	31				

APRIL

S	M	T	W	T	F	S
			1	2	3	4
5	6	7	8	9	10	11
12	13	14	15	16	17	18
19	20	21	22	23	24	25
26	27	28	29	30		

MAY

S	M	T	W	T	F	S
					1	2
3	4	5	6	7	8	9
10	11	12	13	14	15	16
17	18	19	20	21	22	23
24	25	26	27	28	29	30
31						

JUNE

S	M	T	W	T	F	S
	1	2	3	4	5	6
7	8	9	10	11	12	13
14	15	16	17	18	19	20
21	22	23	24	25	26	27
28	29	30				

JULY

S	M	T	W	T	F	S
			1	2	3	4
5	6	7	8	9	10	11
12	13	14	15	16	17	18
19	20	21	22	23	24	25
26	27	28	29	30	31	

AUGUST

S	M	T	W	T	F	S
						1
2	3	4	5	6	7	8
9	10	11	12	13	14	15
16	17	18	19	20	21	22
23	24	25	26	27	28	29
30	31					

SEPTEMBER

S	M	T	W	T	F	S
		1	2	3	4	5
6	7	8	9	10	11	12
13	14	15	16	17	18	19
20	21	22	23	24	25	26
27	28	29	30			

OCTOBER

S	M	T	W	T	F	S
				1	2	3
4	5	6	7	8	9	10
11	12	13	14	15	16	17
18	19	20	21	22	23	24
25	26	27	28	29	30	31

NOVEMBER

S	M	T	W	T	F	S
1	2	3	4	5	6	7
8	9	10	11	12	13	14
15	16	17	18	19	20	21
22	23	24	25	26	27	28
29	30					

DECEMBER

S	M	T	W	T	F	S
		1	2	3	4	5
6	7	8	9	10	11	12
13	14	15	16	17	18	19
20	21	22	23	24	25	26
27	28	29	30	31		

Schema #8

JANUARY

S	M	T	W	T	F	S
			1	2	3	4
5	6	7	8	9	10	11
12	13	14	15	16	17	18
19	20	21	22	23	24	25
26	27	28	29	30	31	

FEBRUARY

S	M	T	W	T	F	S
						1
2	3	4	5	6	7	8
9	10	11	12	13	14	15
16	17	18	19	20	21	22
23	24	25	26	27	28	29

MARCH

S	M	T	W	T	F	S
1	2	3	4	5	6	7
8	9	10	11	12	13	14
15	16	17	18	19	20	21
22	23	24	25	26	27	28
29	30	31				

APRIL

S	M	T	W	T	F	S
			1	2	3	4
5	6	7	8	9	10	11
12	13	14	15	16	17	18
19	20	21	22	23	24	25
26	27	28	29	30		

MAY

S	M	T	W	T	F	S
					1	2
3	4	5	6	7	8	9
10	11	12	13	14	15	16
17	18	19	20	21	22	23
24	25	26	27	28	29	30
31						

JUNE

S	M	T	W	T	F	S
	1	2	3	4	5	6
7	8	9	10	11	12	13
14	15	16	17	18	19	20
21	22	23	24	25	26	27
28	29	30				

JULY

S	M	T	W	T	F	S
			1	2	3	4
5	6	7	8	9	10	11
12	13	14	15	16	17	18
19	20	21	22	23	24	25
26	27	28	29	30	31	

AUGUST

S	M	T	W	T	F	S
						1
2	3	4	5	6	7	8
9	10	11	12	13	14	15
16	17	18	19	20	21	22
23	24	25	26	27	28	29
30	31					

SEPTEMBER

S	M	T	W	T	F	S
		1	2	3	4	5
6	7	8	9	10	11	12
13	14	15	16	17	18	19
20	21	22	23	24	25	26
27	28	29	30			

OCTOBER

S	M	T	W	T	F	S
				1	2	3
4	5	6	7	8	9	10
11	12	13	14	15	16	17
18	19	20	21	22	23	24
25	26	27	28	29	30	31

NOVEMBER

S	M	T	W	T	F	S
1	2	3	4	5	6	7
8	9	10	11	12	13	14
15	16	17	18	19	20	21
22	23	24	25	26	27	28
29	30					

DECEMBER

S	M	T	W	T	F	S
		1	2	3	4	5
6	7	8	9	10	11	12
13	14	15	16	17	18	19
20	21	22	23	24	25	26
27	28	29	30	31		

Schema #9

JANUARY
S	M	T	W	T	F	S
	1	2	3	4	5	6
7	8	9	10	11	12	13
14	15	16	17	18	19	20
21	22	23	24	25	26	27
28	29	30	31			

FEBRUARY
S	M	T	W	T	F	S
				1	2	3
4	5	6	7	8	9	10
11	12	13	14	15	16	17
18	19	20	21	22	23	24
25	26	27	28	29		

MARCH
S	M	T	W	T	F	S
					1	2
3	4	5	6	7	8	9
10	11	12	13	14	15	16
17	18	19	20	21	22	23
24	25	26	27	28	29	30
31						

APRIL
S	M	T	W	T	F	S
	1	2	3	4	5	6
7	8	9	10	11	12	13
14	15	16	17	18	19	20
21	22	23	24	25	26	27
28	29	30				

MAY
S	M	T	W	T	F	S
			1	2	3	4
5	6	7	8	9	10	11
12	13	14	15	16	17	18
19	20	21	22	23	24	25
26	27	28	29	30	31	

JUNE
S	M	T	W	T	F	S
						1
2	3	4	5	6	7	8
9	10	11	12	13	14	15
16	17	18	19	20	21	22
23	24	25	26	27	28	29
30						

JULY
S	M	T	W	T	F	S
	1	2	3	4	5	6
7	8	9	10	11	12	13
14	15	16	17	18	19	20
21	22	23	24	25	26	27
28	29	30	31			

AUGUST
S	M	T	W	T	F	S
				1	2	3
4	5	6	7	8	9	10
11	12	13	14	15	16	17
18	19	20	21	22	23	24
25	26	27	28	29	30	31

SEPTEMBER
S	M	T	W	T	F	S
1	2	3	4	5	6	7
8	9	10	11	12	13	14
15	16	17	18	19	20	21
22	23	24	25	26	27	28
29	30					

OCTOBER
S	M	T	W	T	F	S
		1	2	3	4	5
6	7	8	9	10	11	12
13	14	15	16	17	18	19
20	21	22	23	24	25	26
27	28	29	30	31		

NOVEMBER
S	M	T	W	T	F	S
					1	2
3	4	5	6	7	8	9
10	11	12	13	14	15	16
17	18	19	20	21	22	23
24	25	26	27	28	29	30

DECEMBER
S	M	T	W	T	F	S
1	2	3	4	5	6	7
8	9	10	11	12	13	14
15	16	17	18	19	20	21
22	23	24	25	26	27	28
29	30	31				

Schema #10

JANUARY

S	M	T	W	T	F	S
						1
2	3	4	5	6	7	8
9	10	11	12	13	14	15
16	17	18	19	20	21	22
23	24	25	26	27	28	29
30	31					

FEBRUARY

S	M	T	W	T	F	S
		1	2	3	4	5
6	7	8	9	10	11	12
13	14	15	16	17	18	19
20	21	22	23	24	25	26
27	28	29				

MARCH

S	M	T	W	T	F	S
		1	2	3	4	
5	6	7	8	9	10	11
12	13	14	15	16	17	18
19	20	21	22	23	24	25
26	27	28	29	30	31	

APRIL

S	M	T	W	T	F	S
						1
2	3	4	5	6	7	8
9	10	11	12	13	14	15
16	17	18	19	20	21	22
23	24	25	26	27	28	29
30						

MAY

S	M	T	W	T	F	S
	1	2	3	4	5	6
7	8	9	10	11	12	13
14	15	16	17	18	19	20
21	22	23	24	25	26	27
28	29	30	31			

JUNE

S	M	T	W	T	F	S
				1	2	3
4	5	6	7	8	9	10
11	12	13	14	15	16	17
18	19	20	21	22	23	24
25	26	27	28	29	30	

JULY

S	M	T	W	T	F	S
						1
2	3	4	5	6	7	8
9	10	11	12	13	14	15
16	17	18	19	20	21	22
23	24	25	26	27	28	29
30	31					

AUGUST

S	M	T	W	T	F	S
		1	2	3	4	5
6	7	8	9	10	11	12
13	14	15	16	17	18	19
20	21	22	23	24	25	26
27	28	29	30	31		

SEPTEMBER

S	M	T	W	T	F	S
					1	2
3	4	5	6	7	8	9
10	11	12	13	14	15	16
17	18	19	20	21	22	23
24	25	26	27	28	29	30

OCTOBER

S	M	T	W	T	F	S
1	2	3	4	5	6	7
8	9	10	11	12	13	14
15	16	17	18	19	20	21
22	23	24	25	26	27	28
29	30	31				

NOVEMBER

S	M	T	W	T	F	S
			1	2	3	4
5	6	7	8	9	10	11
12	13	14	15	16	17	18
19	20	21	22	23	24	25
26	27	28	29	30		

DECEMBER

S	M	T	W	T	F	S
					1	2
3	4	5	6	7	8	9
10	11	12	13	14	15	16
17	18	19	20	21	22	23
24	25	26	27	28	29	30
31						

Schema #11

JANUARY

S	M	T	W	T	F	S
				1	2	3
4	5	6	7	8	9	10
11	12	13	14	15	16	17
18	19	20	21	22	23	24
25	26	27	28	29	30	31

FEBRUARY

S	M	T	W	T	F	S
1	2	3	4	5	6	7
8	9	10	11	12	13	14
15	16	17	18	19	20	21
22	23	24	25	26	27	28
29						

MARCH

S	M	T	W	T	F	S
	1	2	3	4	5	6
7	8	9	10	11	12	13
14	15	16	17	18	19	20
21	22	23	24	25	26	27
28	29	30	31			

APRIL

S	M	T	W	T	F	S
				1	2	3
4	5	6	7	8	9	10
11	12	13	14	15	16	17
18	19	20	21	22	23	24
25	26	27	28	29	30	

MAY

S	M	T	W	T	F	S
						1
2	3	4	5	6	7	8
5	6	7	8	9	10	11
12	13	14	15	16	17	18
19	20	21	22	23	24	25
26	27	28	29	30	31	

JUNE

S	M	T	W	T	F	S
	1	2	3	4	5	
6	7	8	9	10	11	12
13	14	15	16	17	18	19
20	21	22	23	24	25	26
27	28	29	30			

JULY

S	M	T	W	T	F	S
				1	2	3
4	5	6	7	8	9	10
11	12	13	14	15	16	17
18	19	20	21	22	23	24
25	26	27	28	29	30	31

AUGUST

S	M	T	W	T	F	S
1	2	3	4	5	6	7
8	9	10	11	12	13	14
15	16	17	18	19	20	21
22	23	24	25	26	27	28
29	30	31				

SEPTEMBER

S	M	T	W	T	F	S
			1	2	3	4
5	6	7	8	9	10	11
12	13	14	15	16	17	18
19	20	21	22	23	24	25
26	27	28	29	30		

OCTOBER

S	M	T	W	T	F	S
					1	2
3	4	5	6	7	8	9
10	11	12	13	14	15	16
17	18	19	20	21	22	23
24	25	26	27	28	29	30
31						

NOVEMBER

S	M	T	W	T	F	S
	1	2	3	4	5	6
7	8	9	10	11	12	13
14	15	16	17	18	19	20
21	22	23	24	25	26	27
28	29	30				

DECEMBER

S	M	T	W	T	F	S
			1	2	3	4
5	6	7	8	9	10	11
12	13	14	15	16	17	18
19	20	21	22	23	24	25
26	27	28	29	30	31	

Schema #12

JANUARY

S	M	T	W	T	F	S
		1	2	3	4	5
6	7	8	9	10	11	12
13	14	15	16	17	18	19
20	21	22	23	24	25	26
27	28	29	30	31		

FEBRUARY

S	M	T	W	T	F	S
					1	2
3	4	5	6	7	8	9
10	11	12	13	14	15	16
17	18	19	20	21	22	23
24	25	26	27	28	29	

MARCH

S	M	T	W	T	F	S
						1
2	3	4	5	6	7	8
9	10	11	12	13	14	15
16	17	18	19	20	21	22
23	24	25	26	27	28	29
30	31					

APRIL

S	M	T	W	T	F	S
		1	2	3	4	5
6	7	8	9	10	11	12
13	14	15	16	17	18	19
20	21	22	23	24	25	26
27	28	29	30			

MAY

S	M	T	W	T	F	S
				1	2	3
4	5	6	7	8	9	10
11	12	13	14	15	16	17
18	19	20	21	22	23	24
25	26	27	28	29	30	31

JUNE

S	M	T	W	T	F	S
1	2	3	4	5	6	7
8	9	10	11	12	13	14
15	16	17	18	19	20	21
22	23	24	25	26	27	28
29	30					

JULY

S	M	T	W	T	F	S
		1	2	3	4	5
6	7	8	9	10	11	12
13	14	15	16	17	18	19
20	21	22	23	24	25	26
27	28	29	30	31		

AUGUST

S	M	T	W	T	F	S
					1	2
3	4	5	6	7	8	9
10	11	12	13	14	15	16
17	18	19	20	21	22	23
24	25	26	27	28	29	30
31						

SEPTEMBER

S	M	T	W	T	F	S
	1	2	3	4	5	6
7	8	9	10	11	12	13
14	15	16	17	18	19	20
21	22	23	24	25	26	27
28	29	30				

OCTOBER

S	M	T	W	T	F	S
			1	2	3	4
5	6	7	8	9	10	11
12	13	14	15	16	17	18
19	20	21	22	23	24	25
26	27	28	29	30	31	

NOVEMBER

S	M	T	W	T	F	S
						1
2	3	4	5	6	7	8
9	10	11	12	13	14	15
16	17	18	19	20	21	22
23	24	25	26	27	28	29
30						

DECEMBER

S	M	T	W	T	F	S
	1	2	3	4	5	6
7	8	9	10	11	12	13
14	15	16	17	18	19	20
21	22	23	24	25	26	27
28	29	30	31			

Schema #13

JANUARY

S	M	T	W	T	F	S
1	2	3	4	5	6	7
8	9	10	11	12	13	14
15	16	17	18	19	20	21
22	23	24	25	26	27	28
29	30	31				

FEBRUARY

S	M	T	W	T	F	S
			1	2	3	4
5	6	7	8	9	10	11
12	13	14	15	16	17	18
19	20	21	22	23	24	25
26	27	28	29			

MARCH

S	M	T	W	T	F	S
				1	2	3
4	5	6	7	8	9	10
11	12	13	14	15	16	17
18	19	20	21	22	23	24
25	26	27	28	29	30	31

APRIL

S	M	T	W	T	F	S
1	2	3	4	5	6	7
8	9	10	11	12	13	14
15	16	17	18	19	20	21
22	23	24	25	26	27	28
29	30					

MAY

S	M	T	W	T	F	S
		1	2	3	4	5
6	7	8	9	10	11	12
13	14	15	16	17	18	19
20	21	22	23	24	25	26
27	28	29	30	31		

JUNE

S	M	T	W	T	F	S
					1	2
3	4	5	6	7	8	9
10	11	12	13	14	15	16
17	18	19	20	21	22	23
24	25	26	27	28	29	30

JULY

S	M	T	W	T	F	S
1	2	3	4	5	6	7
8	9	10	11	12	13	14
15	16	17	18	19	20	21
22	23	24	25	26	27	28
29	30	31				

AUGUST

S	M	T	W	T	F	S
			1	2	3	4
5	6	7	8	9	10	11
12	13	14	15	16	17	18
19	20	21	22	23	24	25
26	27	28	29	30	31	

SEPTEMBER

S	M	T	W	T	F	S
						1
2	3	4	5	6	7	8
9	10	11	12	13	14	15
16	17	18	19	20	21	22
23	24	25	26	27	28	29
30						

OCTOBER

S	M	T	W	T	F	S
	1	2	3	4	5	6
7	8	9	10	11	12	13
14	15	16	17	18	19	20
21	22	23	24	25	26	27
28	29	30	31			

NOVEMBER

S	M	T	W	T	F	S
				1	2	3
4	5	6	7	8	9	10
11	12	13	14	15	16	17
18	19	20	21	22	23	24
25	26	27	28	29	30	

DECEMBER

S	M	T	W	T	F	S
						1
2	3	4	5	6	7	8
9	10	11	12	13	14	15
16	17	18	19	20	21	22
23	24	25	26	27	28	29
30	31					

Schema #14

JANUARY

S	M	T	W	T	F	S
					1	2
3	4	5	6	7	8	9
10	11	12	13	14	15	16
17	18	19	20	21	22	23
24	25	26	27	28	29	30
31						

FEBRUARY

S	M	T	W	T	F	S
	1	2	3	4	5	6
7	8	9	10	11	12	13
14	15	16	17	18	19	20
21	22	23	24	25	26	27
28	29					

MARCH

S	M	T	W	T	F	S
		1	2	3	4	5
6	7	8	9	10	11	12
13	14	15	16	17	18	19
20	21	22	23	24	25	26
27	28	29	30	31		

APRIL

S	M	T	W	T	F	S
					1	2
3	4	5	6	7	8	9
10	11	12	13	14	15	16
17	18	19	20	21	22	23
24	25	26	27	28	29	30

MAY

S	M	T	W	T	F	S
1	2	3	4	5	6	7
8	9	10	11	12	13	14
15	16	17	18	19	20	21
22	23	24	25	26	27	28
29	30	31				

JUNE

S	M	T	W	T	F	S
		1	2	3	4	
5	6	7	8	9	10	11
12	13	14	15	16	17	18
19	20	21	22	23	24	25
26	27	28	29	50		

JULY

S	M	T	W	T	F	S
					1	2
3	4	5	6	7	8	9
10	11	12	13	14	15	16
17	18	19	20	21	22	23
24	25	26	27	28	29	30

AUGUST

S	M	T	W	T	F	S
	1	2	3	4	5	6
7	8	9	10	11	12	13
14	15	16	17	18	19	20
21	22	23	24	25	26	27
28	29	30	31			

SEPTEMBER

S	M	T	W	T	F	S
				1	2	3
4	5	6	7	8	9	10
11	12	13	14	15	16	17
18	19	20	21	22	23	24
25	26	27	28	29	30	

OCTOBER

S	M	T	W	T	F	S
						1
2	3	4	5	6	7	8
9	10	11	12	13	14	15
16	17	18	19	20	21	22
23	24	25	26	27	28	29
30	31					

NOVEMBER

S	M	T	W	T	F	S
		1	2	3	4	5
6	7	8	9	10	11	12
13	14	15	16	17	18	19
20	21	22	23	24	25	26
27	28	29	30			

DECEMBER

S	M	T	W	T	F	S
				1	2	3
4	5	6	7	8	9	10
11	12	13	14	15	16	17
18	19	20	21	22	23	24
25	26	27	28	29	30	31

Appendix 7 – Conversion of 12-Hour AM/PM Time to 24-Hour Military Time	
Since Appendix 4 uses military time, it may be needful for some to refer to the following data. It will allow you to see the relativity of our AM and PM system of timekeeping and military time.	

12-Hour AM/PM Time	24-Hour Military Time
12:00 AM (Midnight)	0:00
1:00 AM	1:00
2:00 AM	2:00
3:00 AM	3:00
4:00 AM	4:00
5:00 AM	5:00
6:00 AM	6:00
7:00 AM	7:00
8:00 AM	8:00
9:00 AM	9:00
10:00 AM	10:00
11:00 AM	11:00
12:00 PM (Noon)	12:00
1:00 PM	13:00
2:00 PM	14:00
3:00 PM	15:00
4:00 PM	16:00
5:00 PM	17:00
6:00 PM	18:00
7:00 PM	19:00
8:00 PM	20:00
9:00 PM	21:00
10:00 PM	22:00
11:00 PM	23:00

Appendix 8 – Which Years Are Leap Years on the Gregorian Calendar?	
Almost every four years, the Gregorian calendar makes an intercalary adjustment by adding one day to the year. This happens during the shortest month of the year, by adding an extra day to the end of February.	
The years that end in 00 must be evenly divisible by 400. The year 2000 was a leap year because it was evenly divisible by 400. The year 2100 will not be a leap year because it is not evenly divisible by 400.	
For the rest of the years (those which do not end with 00), if the year is evenly divisible by 4, it is a leap year. 2004, 2008, 20012, ... 2096 are all leap years, then for the reason stated above, 2100 is not. 2104 will begin a new cycle of every fourth year.	

Appendix 9 – Quarterly Zadokite Calendar Template	
For those of you who might desire to make your own calendar, we have designed a calendar template for a three-month period. Since every quarterly cycle repeats in the same form for sequential quarters, the same template can simply be used four times over the course of a year by making new copies of the original template and filling it in according to the current Gregorian calendar. Please turn to the next page for the template.	

Zadokite 364-Day Calendar Year

Day 1 Sunday	Day 2 Monday	Day 3 Tuesday	Day 4 Wednesday	Day 5 Thursday	Day 6 Friday	Day 7 Sabbath
Months 1, 4, 7, 10						
			1	2	3	4
5	6	7	8	9	10	11
12	13	14	15	16	17	18
19	20	21	22	23	24	25
26	27	28	29	30		
Months 2, 5, 8, 11						
					1	2
3	4	5	6	7	8	9
10	11	12	13	14	15	16
17	18	19	20	21	22	23
24	25	26	27	28	29	30
Months 3, 6, 9, 12						
1	2	3	4	5	6	7
8	9	10	11	12	13	14
15	16	17	18	19	20	21
22	23	24	25	26	27	28
29	30	DOT				

Appendix 10 – Quarterly Zadokite Calendar Template Sample Usage	
The template provided under this Appendix is a sample of how to use the template from Appendix 9.	
It shows what was filled in for the third quarter of the year 2016. It is simply a means for uniting the Zadokite	
calendar with the corresponding Gregorian calendar for any given period. Starting with a new copy of the	
template from Appendix 9 each time, the data can be completed quickly and easily. With the use of all of the	
other Appendices, it can be done even if there is no calendar information easily attainable. We only need to	
know what day it is at present, and the rest of the future dates can be determined. Please turn to the next	
page for the sample template.	

Zadokite 364-Day Calendar Year

Day 1	Day 2	Day 3	Day 4	Day 5	Day 6	Day 7
Sunday	Monday	Tuesday	Wednesday	Thursday	Friday	Sabbath

5777 — 2016 Months 1, 4, (7) 10 Sept. – Oct.

Day 1	Day 2	Day 3	Day 4	Day 5	Day 6	Day 7
			1	2	3	4
			Sept. 21	Sept. 22	Sept. 23	Sept. 24
5	6	7	8	9	10	11
Sept 25	Sept 26	Sept 27	Sept 28	Sept 29	Sept 30	Oct 1
12	13	14	15	16	17	18
Oct 2	Oct 3	Oct 4	Oct 5	Oct 6	Oct 7	Oct 8
19	20	21	22	23	24	25
Oct 9	Oct 10	Oct 11	Oct 12	Oct 13	Oct 14	Oct 15
26	27	28	29	30		
Oct 16	Oct 17	Oct 18	Oct 19	Oct 20		

5777 – 2016 Months 2, 5, (8) 11 Oct. – Nov.

Day 1	Day 2	Day 3	Day 4	Day 5	Day 6	Day 7
					1	2
					Oct 21	Oct 22
3	4	5	6	7	8	9
Oct 23	Oct 24	Oct 25	Oct 26	Oct 27	Oct 28	Oct 29
10	11	12	13	14	15	16
Oct 30	Oct 31	Nov 1	Nov 2	Nov 3	Nov 4	Nov 5
17	18	19	20	21	22	23
Nov 6	Nov 7	Nov 8	Nov 9	Nov 10	Nov 11	Nov 12
24	25	26	27	28	29	30
Nov 13	Nov 14	Nov 15	Nov 16	Nov 17	Nov 18	Nov 19

5777 – 2016 Months 3, 6, (9) 12 Nov. – Dec.

Day 1	Day 2	Day 3	Day 4	Day 5	Day 6	Day 7
1	2	3	4	5	6	7
Nov 20	Nov 21	Nov 22	Nov 23	Nov 24	Nov 25	Nov 26
8	9	10	11	12	13	14
Nov 27	Nov 28	Nov 29	Nov 30	Dec 1	Dec 2	Dec 3
15	16	17	18	19	20	21
Dec 4	Dec 5	Dec 6	Dec 7	Dec 8	Dec 9	Dec 10
22	23	24	25	26	27	28
Dec 11	Dec 12	Dec 13	Dec 14	Dec 15	Dec 16	Dec 17
29	30	DOT				
Dec 18	Dec 19	Dec 20				

Appendix 11 – Zadokite and Gregorian One-Year Calendar Templates
This appendix will provide a template that will enable you to create your own Gregorian calendar from the appropriate Schema from Appendix 6, or to construct your own brief version of a yearly Zadokite calendar. Starting with a fresh template copy each time, the years can be figured far into the future. The first template is the Zadokite, and the second is the Gregorian.   Please turn to the next two pages for the templates.

I						
1	2	3	4	5	6	7

II						
1	2	3	4	5	6	7

III						
1	2	3	4	5	6	7

IV						
1	2	3	4	5	6	7

V						
1	2	3	4	5	6	7

VI						
1	2	3	4	5	6	7

VII						
1	2	3	4	5	6	7

VIII						
1	2	3	4	5	6	7

IX						
1	2	3	4	5	6	7

X						
1	2	3	4	5	6	7

XI						
1	2	3	4	5	6	7

XII						
1	2	3	4	5	6	7

January

Su	M	Tu	W	Th	F	Sa

February

Su	M	Tu	W	Th	F	Sa

March

Su	M	Tu	W	Th	F	Sa

April

Su	M	Tu	W	Th	F	Sa

May

Su	M	Tu	W	Th	F	Sa

June

Su	M	Tu	W	Th	F	Sa

July

Su	M	Tu	W	Th	F	Sa

August

Su	M	Tu	W	Th	F	Sa

September

Su	M	Tu	W	Th	F	Sa

October

Su	M	Tu	W	Th	F	Su

November

Su	M	Tu	W	Th	F	Sa

December

Su	M	Tu	W	Th	F	Sa

Appendix 12 – Zadokite or Gregorian One-Month Calendar Template

The template for this appendix is universal. It will work well to chart a monthly reference for either the Zadokite or the Gregorian calendar, with plenty of room for personal notes. Beginning with a fresh template each month will allow you to enter data and information far into the future. Please turn to the next page for the template.

Month and Year:

1/Sunday	2/Monday	3/Tuesday	4/Wednesday	5/Thursday	6/Friday	7/Sabbath